I0487227

API Security

A guide to building and securing APIs
from the developer team at Okta

Foreword by Les Hazlewood

With chapters by

Lee Brandt

Keith Casey

Randall Degges

Brian Demers

Joël Franusic

Sai Maddali

Matt Raible

API Security

by the Developer Team at Okta

Copyright © 2018 by Okta, Inc.

Published by Okta, Inc. 301 Brannan Street, San Francisco, CA, 94107

ISBN: 978-1-387-78313-7

18132.0036

First Edition

○ ○ ○ ○ ○

Table of Contents

o o o o o

Acknowledgments

The authors of the book in your hands today (physically or digitally) would like to take a moment to thank a few individuals without whom this work would not have been assembled.

First and foremost, thanks to our editors, Okta's own Randall Degges and Keith Casey. Their tireless efforts have increased the quality of our work, while also ensuring its accuracy. Their guidance was invaluable and very much appreciated.

We would like to thank two additional Okta colleagues: Aaron Parecki, for graphic design and formatting of both the print and epub versions of this text; and Lindsay Brunner for project management, encouragement, and generally making all of us sound awesome.

And finally, our thanks to the rest of our Okta family, who supported this project from its inception. We hope you enjoy it!

o o o o o
___

Foreword

by Les Hazlewood

I entered the world of information security almost 20 years ago, as often occurs in our industry, by accident. I was a software engineer excited to be working on a very large software system that was being created for the New York Port Authority - right after 9/11. The system was complex and the problems we were solving were genuinely interesting and intellectually gratifying. And because of our customer, keeping the system and its users secure was of the utmost importance. I went from being somewhat naive about how applications were secured to being thrust into a team that was responsible for securing one of the most important computer systems in the country given events at the time. It made software security very real - in a very concrete in a way I hadn't experienced before. When the project was done, I was proud to have helped in some small way to making New York a safer place.

I learned immensely from that experience, and realized how much technology then and since was advancing at break-neck speeds. The learning curve was really steep and all the while, technology was advancing rapidly, and you constantly had to keep learning. It's easy to forget about security when you've got 20 other things to learn just to get an application out the door! But if I take a step back and look at our industry with a wider perspective, I can't help but be intrigued by this exponential growth and innovation - and how security will always play a part.

Humanity has always had the drive to innovate, but we've also been determined to undermine our own advancements for selfish gain through surreptitious means. As a result, it is incumbent on us, the builders and innovators of the world, to protect ourselves. From the Mesopotamian potter 3500 years ago who wanted to keep his glazing techniques secret from competitors to modern banks who safeguard the world's digital financial transactions - there has always been a need to keep information secret. And there have always been people trying to steal those secrets.

What's important about this dichotomic dance between information holder and information thief is that the dance never ends - a safeguard today will eventually be bypassed tomorrow, which then must be be supplanted by a better safeguard. Unfortunately, even smart, capable people and corporations forget this or even ignore it, which is why we have the Equifax and Yahoo data breaches of the world.

So what does this mean in the current climate of exploding connectivity between millions of devices in the world, and the HTTP APIs that are shared and consumed between them?

To put it simply, it's the Wild West out there!

Of course, no one expects you to wear leather chaps and ride a horse to work (but if that's your thing, you do you, and do it proudly!), but we software developers are constantly looking down the barrel of a hacker's metaphorical six-shooter.

And while a bit tongue-in-cheek, the Wild West metaphor is valid - the Western frontier in the United States' early years was expanding and changing quickly, and law enforcement often wasn't available. Individuals and companies had to protect themselves using the best strategies and technologies at their disposal. Similarly, our computer and information technology industry is soberingly new - the first digital computer was invented only 70 years ago, in the time of a single human life span! Our still-nascent industry clearly reflects the same opportunity to expand and build, and for some, to engage in nefarious activity.

So what about us? The web and mobile application developers? The API developers? How do we address this expanding frontier when even massive companies fall victim every day?

I believe the answer is that we be smart, informed, and proactive. We focus on known best practices and never stop looking for new ones. We implement modern approaches that have been proven successful in real, practical experience. We stay diligent and learn from those who have come before us, thus standing on the shoulders of giants, like the authors of the book in your hands right now.

So you don't have to be afraid of the Wild West. There are amazing opportunities ahead and the Internet is still the Great Equalizer for today's builders and innovators. And for the API builders among you? Armed with the wonderful information in this book, I'm confident you'll be ahead of (and safer than) 99% of all other APIs today.

Head 'em up, move 'em out!

x

Chapter 1

Transport Layer Security

By Randall Degges

Any discussion of API security, and more broadly security online, has to start with an understanding of Transport Layer Security (TLS) and its cryptographic underpinnings. Transport security adds privacy and integrity for messages between two parties. In common usage, it's the ability to transmit data over a network without exposing that data to untrusted third parties.

Transport security is critical to modern internet infrastructure, where machines on the public internet exchange sensitive data such as passwords, personal information, financial transactions and classified material. Without efficient and effective transport security, these transactions would be tedious or impossible to complete over a shared network.

The rest of this book dives into detail about best practices for securing your APIs. This chapter focuses on the necessary first step of being able to communicate securely over a network. We'll also cover common pitfalls and best practices for securing your data in transit.

A Brief History of Secure Data Transport

Today we take for granted our ability to send data over the internet securely. When we purchase an item from Amazon or complete our taxes online, we place our trust in the infrastructure of the internet to securely share our data with only the systems and parties we intend.

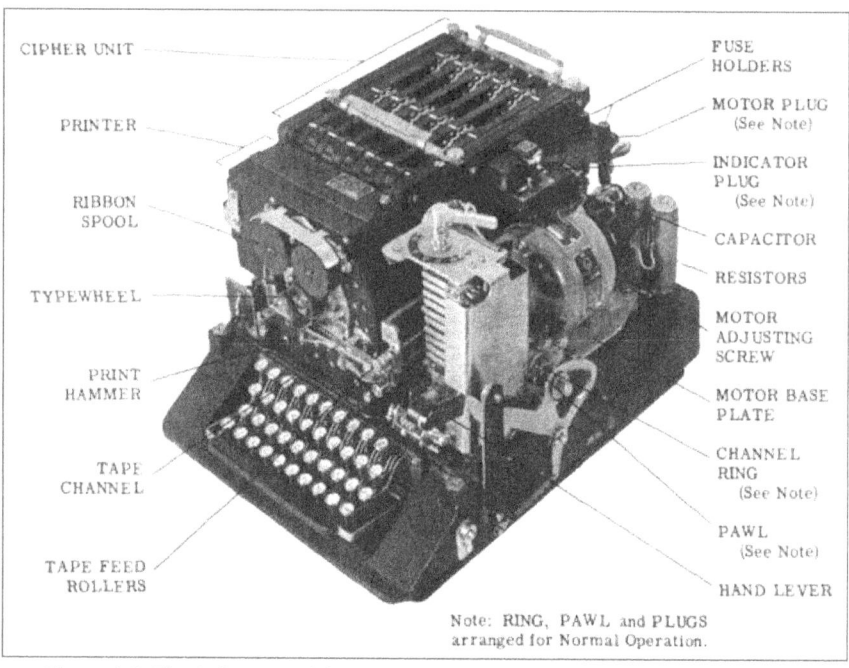

CIPHER UNIT
PRINTER
RIBBON SPOOL
TYPEWHEEL
PRINT HAMMER
TAPE CHANNEL
TAPE FEED ROLLERS

FUSE HOLDERS
MOTOR PLUG (See Note)
INDICATOR PLUG (See Note)
CAPACITOR
RESISTORS
MOTOR ADJUSTING SCREW
MOTOR BASE PLATE
CHANNEL RING (See Note)
PAWL (See Note)
HAND LEVER

Note: RING, PAWL and PLUGS arranged for Normal Operation.

Figure 1-1: The SIGABA, a cipher machine used by the US during World War II

Historically, secure information exchange wasn't simple. Ciphers and cryptography were used in ancient times to encode sensitive messages. These schemes generally had to two main weaknesses: they relied on a shared code book or cipher to encode/decode the messages, and third parties could decode them through pattern analysis.

The problem of a shared code book or cipher persisted for millennia. To ensure that each party would be able to encode/ decode the message successfully, a secret "key" needs to be exchanged, for example by courier or diplomatic bag. By working off the same key, the parties to the message exchange would then be able to encode/decode their data. However, if a nefarious actor were able to gain access to the secret key (for example, by bribing the courier) then all past and future communication could be compromised.

How Key Exchange Works Today

Current hybrid cryptosystems like SSL/TLS use symmetric key algorithms (they are generally faster than asymmetric algorithms.) Symmetric key algorithms require a shared secret, exchanged via key-exchange algorithm.

The most famous cryptographic protocol for key exchange is Diffie–Hellman, published in 1976 by Whitfield Diffie and Martin Hellman. Diffie–Hellman allows the creation of a shared secret between a sender and receiver. This shared secret is unable to be deduced by an eavesdropper who is observing the messages between the sender and receiver, except via a brute force attack. If the keyspace for the shared secret is large enough and the secret generated is sufficiently random, brute force attacks become nearly impossible.

Acronym Party: HTTPS/SSL/TLS

Now that we're up to speed on the basics of key exchange, let's discuss some of the acronyms you'll see throughout this discussion:

- HTTPS, also called HTTP over SSL/TLS, is an extension of HTTP which encrypts communication. HTTPS URLs begin with "https://" and use port 443 by default. This is an improvement over HTTP, which is vulnerable to eavesdropping and man-in-the-middle attacks.
- SSL or Secure Sockets Layer was released by Netscape in 1995. SSL adoption increased after the redesigned SSL 3.0 was released in 1996. The IETF prohibited SSL 2.0 in 2011. SSL 3.0 was prohibited in 2015 after the IETF identified various security vulnerabilities which affected all SSL 3.0

ciphers.

- TLS or Transport Layer Security is the successor to SSL. In fact, the documentation for TLS 1.0 describes it as an "upgrade" of SSL 3.0. The current TLS version is 1.3. Although virtually all HTTPS-secured traffic uses TLS due to problems with SSL, the SSL nomenclature persists in internet culture. These days, when somebody says SSL, it is likely they mean TLS.

In this article, I use "SSL/TLS" to avoid ambiguity that the term SSL causes. However, your implementations should always use TLS.

Establishing a SSL/TLS Session

When an SSL/TLS connection needs to be made between a client (a browser, or an application attempting to access an API) and a server (a web server, for example, or an API endpoint) it follows a number of steps. The TLS spec, published by the IETF Transport Layer Security Working Group, gives an overview of these steps.

In Figure 1-2 we show a visual representation of how the client or "sender" and server or "receiver" set up an SSL/TLS connection.

Let's walk through the steps at a high level:

TCP Connection

Your client (browser or application) will initiate a TCP connection with the server. Your client and server can exchange information once this connection is established. Although TLS can work over different transports, by far the most common use case is over TCP/IP, due to its ubiquity, reliability of transport and ability to recover from lost packets and transport errors. In the diagram, SYN, SYN ACK, and ACK denote this sequence of events.

SSL/TLS Handshake

The SSL/TLS handshake takes place once a TCP connection is established.

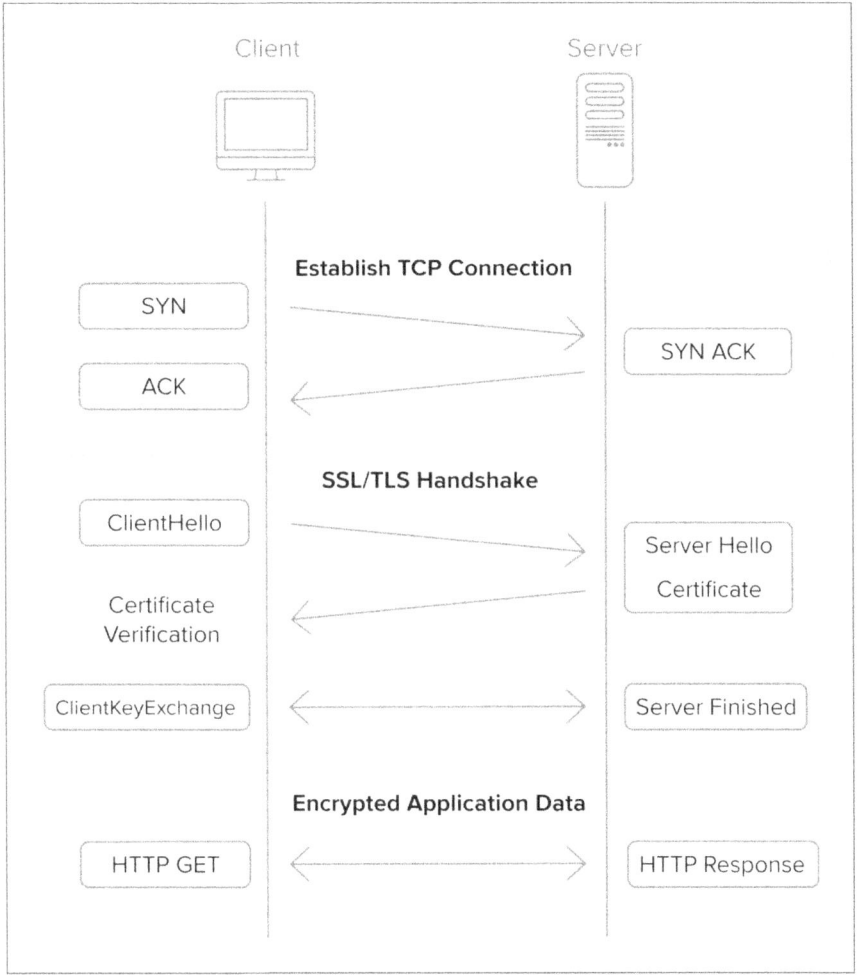

Figure 1-2: TLS Sequence Diagram

ClientHello

The client sends a "ClientHello" message, which lists the versions of SSL/TLS the client is capable of, what ciphersuites it has available, and any compression types available.

ServerHello and Certificate Response

The server responds with the same information as the client, and sends the server's certificate back to the client as well.

Certificate Verification

The client verifies that the certificate is valid, and also verifies that the server is authentic and not an impersonator conducting a man-in-the-middle attack. For more information about how certificate verification is accomplished, see "SSL/TLS Certificate Verification" later in this chapter.

ClientKeyExchange

In the previous section, we discussed key exchange, with the example Diffie–Hellman algorithm. This is the step of the handshake where the key exchange actually happens.

Finished/Application Data

Now that the handshake has been established and keys have been exchanged, information may be encrypted and decrypted between the client and server based on the shared secret which has been generated. This symmetric cryptography will secure the remainder of application-to-application communication.

Exposed Data over SSL/TLS

TLS aims to provide data integrity and privacy between two trusted parties. Information exchanged over the latest version of TLS should be secure from being exposed to third parties in unencrypted form. Additionally, third parties should be unable to modify that information: this is the concept of data integrity, and is the reason an integrity check is performed on each message.

However, even though application data transmitted over a properly-established TLS connection is secure, some metadata and connection information is necessarily exposed to third parties.

Without additional obfuscation outside of the scope of SSL/TLS, an observer will be able to discover:

- **The IP addresses of the client and server.** Since the client and server are communicating over TCP/IP, which operates at a lower level than the TLS protocol, these IP addresses are public and are used for routing the encrypted packets.
- **The server certificate**, including the server name. Since the server sends the certificate to the client as a part of the handshake process before encrypted messages are sent, an observer of the handshake will see the certificate in plain text.
- **The approximate length of the URL and payload.** Although the application data is encrypted, an astute observer of an HTTPS connection will be able to deduce the length of the URL requested and the approximate size of any non-cached assets. Cached assets, since they reside on the client already, are not vulnerable to this introspection until the cache expires and they are re-fetched.

In addition to the data listed above, additional information may be inferred based on the timing of network requests. Outdated SSL/TLS versions have additional identified vulnerabilities, and in the future one must anticipate the TLS spec will be versioned to ameliorate any vulnerabilities identified in the future.

Server Certificates

You've seen that SSL/TLS server certificates are integral to the SSL/TLS handshake. They help the client verify that the server is who they appear to be, which helps prevent third parties impersonating the server. But what are certificates, anyway? How are they generated, and why do the clients trust them?

SSL/TLS Server Certificates are small data files that encapsulate information about the server that owns the certificate. This information is verified through a chain of Certificate Authorities that bridge the gap between the authorities that the browser trusts and the authorities that trust the server.

Certificate Generation

Private or self-signed SSL/TLS certificates are trivial to create. OpenSSL, available for most platforms, allows users to create self-signed SSL/TLS certificates. These consist of a private key and a public key, which a client and server can use to encrypt data and exchange it securely.

The downside to self-signed certificates are that they provide no guarantees of the server's identity. This may not be an issue for corporate networks, where certificates can be exchanged and trusted through internal provisioning.

Trusted Certificates

If anybody can create and self-sign their own certificate, then how is a client (be it a browser or an application hitting an API endpoint) able to verify a server's identity?

On the public internet, trusted certificates are required. Historically, generating these trusted certificates could be expensive. Trust and identity on the web works similarly to meeting individuals in the real world. If somebody wants to verify your identity in person, they may ask for a photo ID generated by a trusted third party, like a government, school or corporate institution. The person verifying your identity trusts that this third party has verified your identity and that your ID cannot be forged.

This is called a chain of trust, and certificates are verified on the web in the same way. Each client has a list of third parties that they trust to verify certificates. These are called root certificate authorities. Microsoft, Oracle, Mozilla, Adobe and Apple maintain lists of trusted root certificate authorities through their own root programs and include these lists in the operating systems and browsers they produce.

Recently there has been an effort to spread adoption of HTTPS by making generating and installing certificates as easy as possible. Amazon Certificate Manager *(https://aws.amazon.com/certificate-manager/)* and Let's Encrypt *(https://letsencrypt.org/)* are two certificate authorities who make it easy to create and manage trusted certificates for free.

Certificate Verification

Now that we understand the importance of trusted certificates and why certificate authorities are necessary, let's walk through the missing middle step: how a client verifies a server's SSL/TLS certificate.

First, the client gets the server's certificate as part of the SSL/TLS handshake. (If you are writing an application that is hitting an HTTPS API endpoint, this step happens before any application data is exchanged.)

The client checks to ensure that the server's certificate is not expired and that the domain name or IP address on the certificate matches the server's information. Then, the client attempts to verify that the server's certificate has been properly signed by the certificate authority who authorized it. Due to the nature of asymmetric encryption, the client is able to do this using the information within the server's response -- without even contacting the certificate authority.

It's unlikely that the server's certificate is signed directly by a root certificate authority that is trusted by the client. However, the client can trust any number of intermediate certificate authorities, as long as the trust chain eventually leads back to one of the client's trusted root certificates, as illustrated in Figure 1-3.

For each intermediate certificate, the client completes the same process: it verifies the issuer's name matches the certificate owner's name, and uses the signature and public key to verify that the certificate is properly signed.

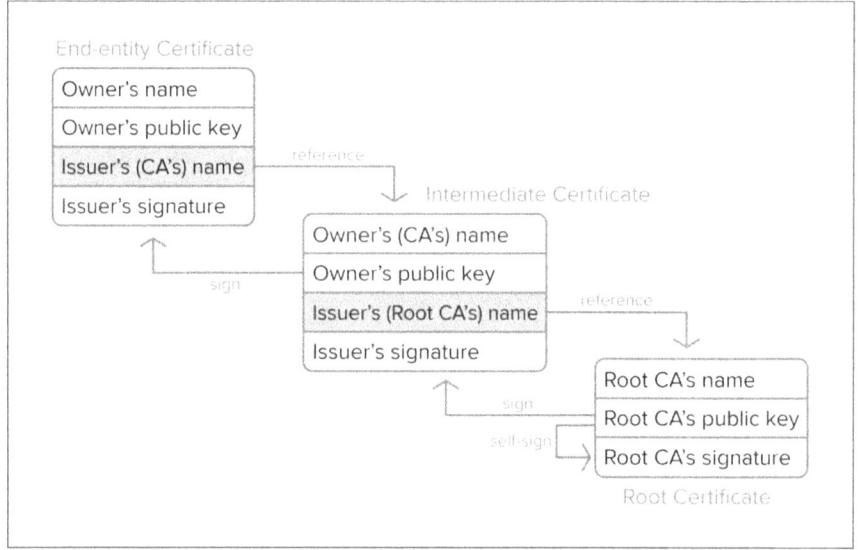

Figure 1-3: Illustrating the chain of trust from a root CA through an intermediate certificate

Eventually, in a successful transaction, the client will come to a self-signed root certificate that the client implicitly trusts. At this point, the client has built a cryptographic chain of trust to the server, and the SSL/TLS handshake can proceed.

Best Practices

Hopefully this chapter has convinced you of the ease and importance of implementing SSL/TLS into your public internet application infrastructure. However, even when using SSL/TLS, organizations can be subject to compromise if best practices are not followed. Let's go over a few of the big ones:

1. Use TLS Everywhere

Having certain pages served over SSL/TLS and some served unencrypted can expose data, such as unencrypted session IDs, to attackers. Similarly, don't allow TLS content to be exposed via non-TLS pages and don't mix TLS and non-TLS content on the same page.

2. Keep Sensitive Data out of the URL and Cache

URLs can be cached in a client's browser history or application logs and sent to another HTTPS site if the user clicks on a link. Setting TLS pages to be uncacheable prevents information leakage from the client cache.

3. Prevent Exposed Data over SSL/TLS

Ensure browsers and applications only access your site via HTTPS by enacting HTTP Strict Transport Security (HSTS). Servers utilizing HSTS send an HTTPS header in their response specifying that requests to their domain should only use HTTPS. An HSTS-complaint client should then make all future requests to that domain over HTTPS, even if HTTP is specified. This helps protect clients from man-in-the-middle and eavesdropping attacks that could be initiated by the client sending sensitive information by making an unsecure HTTP request. For more information, see *https://www.owasp.org/index.php/ HTTP_Strict_Transport_Security_Cheat_Sheet.*

4. Use HTTP Public Key Pinning

While not common in browser-to-web-server communications, HTTP Public Key Pinning is quite useful in API communication. The server will respond with an HTTP header specifying a hash of a valid public key, which helps combat certificate authority compromises. When communicating between two server-side apps, if one server has been compromised and an untrusted certificate authority is trusted, TLS compromise can happen. By having the client download and store a known-valid certificate from the server, the client can "skip" the chain-of-trust verification and instead compare the server's certificate directly to their known-good version, thereby guaranteeing authenticity and preventing any opportunity for man-in-the-middle.

5. Only Support Strong Protocols and Ciphers

Ensure your infrastructure uses the most recent stable version of TLS and the latest recommended ciphers. Due to evolving vulnerabilities, preferred ciphers may change over time.

OWASP maintains a nearly definitive list of best practices for SSL/TLS online at *https://www.owasp.org/index.php/Transport_Layer_Protection_Cheat_Sheet*.

SSL Rating

After implementing SSL/TLS into your API endpoint infrastructure, be sure to run an SSL Rating test to validate your use of the SSL/TLS Best Practices in the section above. While an A+ SSL rating is not a guarantee that your infrastructure is ideally provisioned, any lower rating should raise red flags that you can correct.

To run the SSL Rating test on your public-facing site, visit *https://www.ssllabs.com/ssltest*.

Even if you aren't interested in learning about Diffie-Hellman or Certificate Authorities, you still need to secure your API using TLS/SSL and follow the best practices above.

However, I do encourage you to learn more about the details of TLS/SSL. It can be a daunting task and seemingly never-ending task sometimes, but as with any technology, the more you know about TLS/SSL, the more effective you'll be at building, testing, and reasoning about using it to secure your API. While once could fill an entire book about this topic, hopefully this chapter helped you learn more about the basics of TLS/SSL or helped fill in some gaps in your knowledge.

Chapter 2

DOS Mitigation Strategies

By Lee Brandt

Unfortunately, there's no way to *completely* prevent Denial of Service (DoS) attacks. And that's a problem because they're a plague upon our industry. Between botnets consisting of 6 to 30 million bots *(https://themerkle.com/top-4-largest-botnets-to-date)*, 30,000 distinct DoS attacks per year and growing *(https://www.securityweek.com/internet-sees-nearly-30000-distinct-dos-attacks-each-day-study)*, and 11.2 billion connected "things" in use by the end of 2018 *(https://www.gartner.com/newsroom/id/3598917)*, this problem is only going to get worse. As a developer, the only thing you can do is attempt to mitigate the probability and effectiveness of an attack. So, how do you do that? First, you have to understand what a Denial of Service attack is.

What Is a DoS Attack?

A Denial of Service attack occurs when attackers attempt to stop a service from servicing the requests of legitimate users. Most commonly, this is done by flooding the service with requests until it is no longer able to respond as fast as the requests are coming in. By forcing the service to respond to the flood of requests continually, the service denies legitimate traffic.

Why are DoS Attacks So Prevalent?

There are several reasons why someone might perform a DoS attack on a network or service. Most frequently, DoS attacks are carried out for profit. There are several ways to make money by staging a DoS attack. For instance, competitors of Amazon might find it beneficial if Amazon's service were slow or offline. This form of industrial sabotage may encourage customers to search for alternatives, increasing profits for competing businesses who aren't suffering the effects of a DoS attack.

Another way attackers can profit from DoS attacks is by selling access to compromised computers (called "BotNets") that can perform large-scale Distributed Denial of Service (DDoS) attacks. There are many places online where people can contract BotNets to carry out DDoS attacks. They can typically be rented and charge based on the amount of time that they slow or disable the target service; costs range from a few dollars for a fifteen-minute attack, to a few hundred dollars for twenty-four hours. Portals known as "booter" portals offer the BotNets for hire.

Yet another way attackers can make money by performing an attack is by hijacking personal information like credit cards and social security numbers during a DoS attack. For instance, if attackers target a payment provider with a DoS attack, they might be able to take advantage of the broken system to exploit a vulnerability that isn't available under normal circumstances.

It may also be the case that instead of *making* money from a DoS attack, attackers want to cause their targets monetary losses. For instance, if you write an API that sends SMS messages using a service, you might have to pay a few cents per message sent. If attackers flood your service with a hundred thousand API calls that trigger those SMS messages, the financial loss could be severe.

Also, if an attacker knows that a service provider pays for inbound bandwidth, it might just be a matter of sending the service far more (or larger) requests than normal to eat up available bandwidth resources, causing the victim's cloud provider to send them a hefty monthly bill. Even a few calls made to a particularly data-heavy service can increase a company's cloud-based bandwidth costs. For instance, if a website hosts many large video files, repeatedly downloading massive video files will quickly drive up the provider's bandwidth costs.

Finally, an attack might be carried out for political reasons. This type of attack is akin to a political protest where protesters might block the door of a business that offends their political sensibilities. In 2011, a group known as the Syrian Electronic Army *(https://www.cnn.com/2013/04/24/tech/syrian-electronic-army/ index.html)* worked to support the government of Syrian President Bashar al-Assad by targeting political opposition groups. In October of last year, the Czech Parliamentary election was the target of an attack *(https://sputniknews.com/europe/201710231058456317-czech- election-hit-cyberattack/)* meant to disrupt the counting of votes. Given all these motivations, it's easy to see why so many API services come under attack.

Types of Denial of Service Attacks

There are three main types of DoS attacks:

1. Application-layer Flood

In this attack type, an attacker simply floods the service with requests from a spoofed IP address in an attempt to slow or crash the service, illustrated in Figure 2-1. This could take the form of millions of requests per second or a few thousand requests to a particularly resource-intensive service that eat up resources until the service is unable to continue processing the requests.

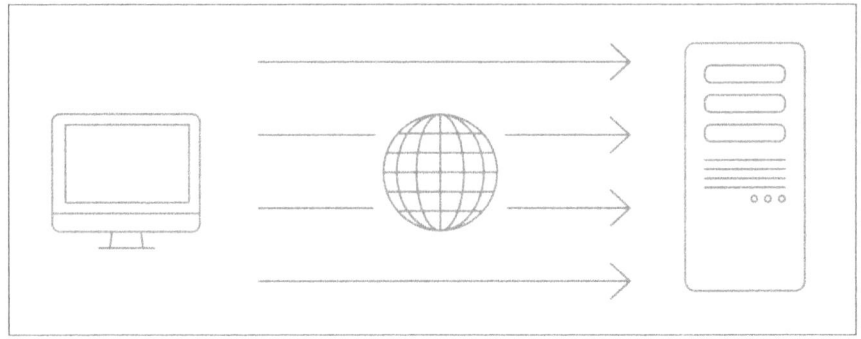

Figure 2-1: An attacker floods the service from a single IP address

Preventing application-layer DoS attacks can be tricky. The best way to help mitigate these types of attacks is to outsource pattern detection and IP filtering to a third party (discussed later).

2. Distributed Denial of Service Attacks (DDoS)

Distributed Denial of Service (DDoS) attacks occur in much the same way as DoS attacks except that requests are sent from many clients as opposed to just one, illustrated in Figure 2-2. DDoS attacks often involve many "zombie" machines (machines that have been previously compromised and are being controlled by attackers). These "zombie" machines then send massive amounts of requests to a service to disable it.

DDoS attacks are famously hard to mitigate, which is why outsourcing network filtering to a third party is the recommended approach. We'll cover this later on.

3. Unintended Denial of Service Attacks

Not all DoS attacks are nefarious. The third attack type is the "unintended" Denial of Service attack. The canonical example of an unintended DDoS is called "The Slashdot Effect *(https://hup.hu/old/stuff/slashdotted/SlashDotEffect.html)*". Slashdot is an internet news site where anyone can post news stories and link to other sites. If a linked story becomes popular, it can cause millions of users to visit the site overloading the site with requests. If the site isn't built to handle that kind of load, the increased traffic can slow or even crash the linked site. Reddit and "The Reddit Hug of Death (*https://thenextweb.com/socialmedia/2012/01/17/how-reddit-turned-one-congressional-candidates-campaign-upside-down/*)" is another excellent example of an unintentional DoS.

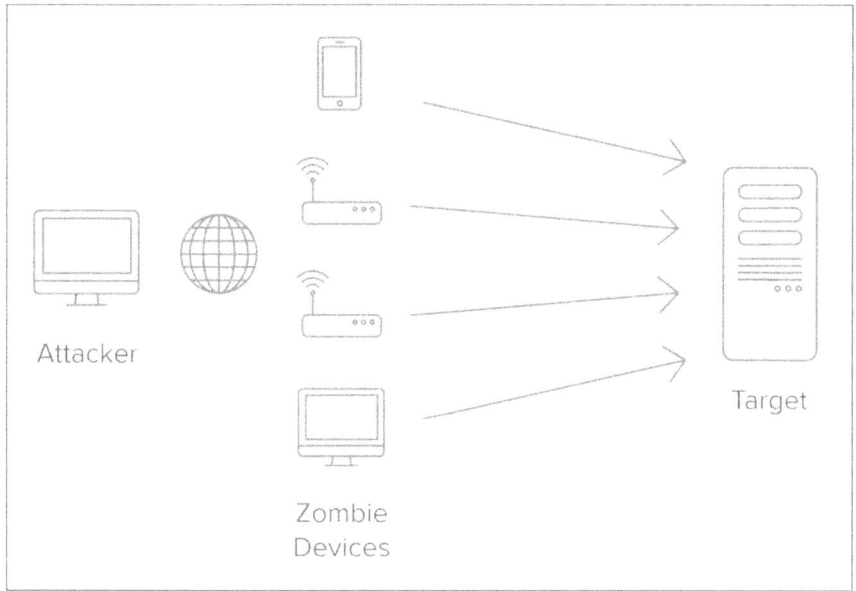

Figure 2-2: An attacker uses zombie machines to launch a DDoS against the target

The only way to prevent these types of unintended DoS attacks is to architect your application for scale. Use patterns like edge-caching with CDNs, HTTP caching headers, auto-scaling groups, and other methods to ensure that even when you receive a large amount of burst-traffic, your site will not go down.

Another type of unintentional DoS attack can occur when servicing low bandwidth areas. For instance, streaming content internationally means that people in certain areas of the world with slow or bad internet connections might cause problems. When your service attempts to send information to these low-bandwidth areas, packets drop. In an attempt to get the information to the destination, your service will attempt to resend all dropped packets. If the connection drops the packets again, your service may make another attempt. This cycle can cause your service's load to double or triple, causing your service to be slow or unreachable for everyone.

How to Mitigate DoS Attacks

Now that you know what DoS attacks are and why attackers perform them, let's discuss how you can protect yourself and your services. Most common mitigation techniques work by detecting illegitimate traffic and blocking it at the routing level, managing and analyzing the bandwidth of the services, and being mindful when architecting your APIs, so they're able to handle large amounts of traffic.

Attack Detection

The first step of any mitigation strategy is understanding when you are the target of a DoS attack. Analyzing incoming traffic and determining whether or not it's legitimate is the first step in keeping your service available and responsive. Scalable cloud service providers are great (and may even "absorb" a DoS attack transparently) which is fantastic until you receive an enormous bill for bandwidth or resource overuse. Making sure your cloud provider makes scaling decisions based only on legitimate traffic is the best way to ensure your company is not spending unnecessary elasticity dollars due to an attack. Early detection of an attack dramatically increases the efficacy of any mitigation strategy.

IP Whitelisting/Blacklisting

The simplest defense against a DoS attack is either whitelisting only legitimate IP addresses or blocking ones from known attackers. For instance, if the application is meant to be used only by employees of a specific company, a hardware or software rule could be created to disallow any traffic, not from a specific IP range. For example, 192.168.0.0/16 would allow any IP address between 192.168.0.0 and 192.168.255.255. The rule rejects any IP address outside that range. If the software is only meant to be used by US citizens, a rule could be created only to allow access to US IP addresses. Inversely, IP blacklisting adds a rule to reject traffic from specific IP addresses or IP ranges making it possible to create rules to disallow traffic coming from China or Russia.

It is important to remember that blocking IP addresses in this way may prevent legitimate traffic from those countries. Blacklisting IP addresses is also dangerous in that you may end up blacklisting all users sharing an IP address, even if many of those users are legitimate. For example, what would happen if a bad actor used an Amazon EC2 server instance to attack a host and that host blocked all Amazon EC2 IP addresses? While the attack might stop, all legitimate Amazon users are now blacklisted from accessing the service.

Also, this strategy may not be effective against DDoS attacks or DoS attacks using spoofed IP addresses. In the distributed scenario, there may be zombie computers with IP addresses all over the place. Creating a rule to filter them out may become complicated and untenable. For instance, if an attacker is generating many requests to your service using a single spoofed IP address, when you block that address the attacker can start spoofing a new IP address and continue the attack.

Rate Limiting

Rate limiting is the practice of limiting the amount of traffic available to a specific Network Interface Controller (NIC). It can be done at the hardware or software level to mitigate the chances of falling victim to a DoS attack. At the hardware level, switches and routers usually have some degree of rate-limiting capabilities. At the software level, it's essential to have a limit on the number of concurrent calls available to a specific customer. Giving users strictly defined limits on concurrent requests or total requests over a given duration (50 requests per minute) can be an excellent way to reject traffic and maintain service stability. The rate limit is usually tied to the customer's plan or payment level. For example, customers on a free plan may only get 1,000 API calls, whereas customers at the premium level may get 10,000 API calls. Once the user reaches their rate limit, the service returns an HTTP status code indicating "too many requests" (status code 429).

While rate limiting is useful, depending on it alone is not enough. Using a router's rate limiting features means that requests will still reach the router. Even the best routers can be overwhelmed and DoSed. At the software level, requests still need to reach your service even if a rate-limit has been reached to serve up a 429 status code. This means that your service could still be overwhelmed by requests, even if your service is only returning an error status code.

Upstream Filtering and DDS

One of the best mitigation strategies is to filter requests upstream, long before it reaches the target network. Done effectively, your API never even sees this traffic, so any rate limiting policies are not triggered. There are many providers of "Mitigation Centers" that will filter the incoming network traffic. For example Amazon Shield *(https://aws.amazon.com/shield/)* and Cloudflare *(https://www.cloudflare.com/)* both offer products that allow for protection against DoS and DDoS attacks by checking incoming packet IPs against known attackers and BotNets and attempt to only forward legitimate traffic. Various API gateways have the same capabilities but can also filter based on the requested endpoint, allowed HTTP verbs, or even a combination of verbs and endpoints.

Passing DoS mitigation responsibility to upstream providers can be a great way to reduce liability and risk as mitigation can be incredibly complex and is an ever-changing cat-and-mouse game between service providers and attackers.

These companies typically offer support should your service be currently under attack in an attempt to minimize damages. It then becomes the responsibility of the provider to keep abreast of new DDoS attack vectors and strategies, leaving you to focus on building your service.

Programming for Scale

With the proliferation of easily-scalable cloud services, it's easy to become lazy and not think about efficient development patterns. Sometimes it's easy to spot DoS-vulnerable parts of your application while other times it's not so apparent. It's vital to offload resource-intensive processes to systems that are designed to handle those operations. In some cases, you may even be able to queue expensive work for later batch processing, reducing DoS attack surface area. For instance, uploading or encoding images or video can take a lot of processing power, and it's essential that your application is not affected by those processes. In some cases, a well-configured cache — at the network or application level — can return data previously processed and unchanged. After all, the fastest processing possible is the processing you don't have to perform.

Sometimes, when a startup is first creating their product, the team pays less attention to performance and more attention to shipping features. While this can be okay early on, as a service becomes popular, it's hard to go back and fix performance issues before they cause a widened surface area for attackers. It's good practice to make performance testing part of the development cycle and continuous integration process. By running the Apache Bench command *(https://httpd.apache.org/docs/2.4/programs/ab.html)*, you can get basic performance information about your service. You can also use AB to write automated tests that simulate many users and check that your service responds to requests within a specified time.

These performance tests can be run during the continuous integration process to ensure the application code performs at a level that is satisfactory to your organization.

Parting Shots

API services are becoming a more and more critical part of the overall world economy, and attacks on API services is on the rise. Whether your services are targeted for fun, profit, or political reasons, it's important to know how to protect your assets (and those of your customers). Mitigating the technological and economic effects of a DoS on your internet-based resources is critical to the success of your company's platform.

Using techniques like IP whitelisting and blacklisting, upstream filtering, rate limiting, and good programming practices is your best defense against would-be attackers. It's important to keep abreast of changes in the security landscape and to make performance and load testing a part of your everyday software delivery practices. Whenever possible, offload the responsibility to companies that specialize in those practices so that you can focus on delivering value to your customers.

Overall, build great stuff… and be careful out there!

Sanitizing Data

By Brian Demers

The inputs to your application represent the most significant surface area of attack for any application. Does your API power forms for user input? Do you display data that didn't originate in your API? Do users upload files through your API?

Any time data crosses a trust boundary - the boundary between any two systems - it should be validated and handled with care. For example, a trust boundary would be any input from an HTTP request, data returned from a database, or calls to remote APIs.

Let's start with a simple example: a user submission to the popular internet forum, Reddit. A user could try to include a malicious string in a comment such as:

```
<img src onerror='alert("haxor")'>
```

If this were rendered as is, in an HTML page, it would pop up an annoying message to the user. However, to get around this, when Reddit displays the text to the user, it is escaped:

```
&lt;img src onerror=&#39;alert(&quot;haxor&quot;)&#39;&gt;
```

which will make the comment appear as visible text instead of HTML, as shown in Figure 3-1.

Figure 3-1: Reddit properly escapes user input

In this example the trust boundary is obvious as any user input should not be trusted.

There are a few different approaches you can use when validating input:

- Accept known good
- Reject bad
- Sanitize
- Do nothing

Accept Known Good

The known good strategy is often the easiest and most foolproof of the given options. With this approach each input is validated against an expected type and format:

- Data type, (Integers are Integers, booleans are booleans, etc)
- Numeric values fall within an expected range (for example: a person's age is always greater than 0 and less than 150)

Chapter 3: Sanitizing Data

- Field length is checked
- Specially formatted string fields such as zipcode, phone number, and social security number are valid

Most web frameworks have some type of declarative support to validate input fields built in. For example, in the Node.js world you can use the popular `validator` package to validate different types of input:

```
import validator from 'validator';
validator.isEmail('foobar@example.com');
```

Reject Bad Inputs

Rejecting known invalid inputs is more complicated than only accepting known good inputs (which we talked about above) and far less accurate. This strategy is typically implemented as a blacklist of strings or patterns. This technique may require many regular expressions to be run against a single field which may also affect the speed of your application. It also means that this blacklist will require updates any time a new pattern needs to be blocked.

Take a typical use-case of blocking 'bad-words'. This problem is incredibly complex as language usage varies across locale. These complexities can be demonstrated using the simple word: ass. It would be pretty easy to block this word alone, but doing so would also block the proper use of the word referring to donkeys. Then you need to think about both variations of the word and where those letters happen to come together: 'badass,' 'hard-ass,' 'amass,' 'bagasse', the first two are questionable while the second two are fine. Even if you block all of these and the thousands of other words that contain these three letters, there are still variations that would make it past: '4ss', 'as.s,' 'azz,' '@ss,' 'āss,' or '\41\73\73' (escaped characters). As time goes on the list of blocked words would increase raising the total cost of the solution.

Another famous example of this technique is antivirus software. Your antivirus updates every few days to get a new blacklist of items to scan. And we all know how well that works ;)

Sanitize Inputs

Sanitizing inputs can be a good option when the input format is not strict but still somewhat predictable, such as phone numbers or other free-text fields. There are a few different ways to sanitize inputs, you could use a whitelist, a blacklist, or escape input.

Sanitize Input Using a Whitelist

When sanitizing data with a whitelist, only valid characters/strings matching a given pattern are kept. For example, when validating a phone number there are multiple formats people use, US phone numbers could be written as `555-123-1245`, `(555) 123-1245`, `555.123.1245`, or a similar combination. Running any of these through a whitelist that only allows numeric characters would leave `5551231245`.

Sanitize Input Using a Blacklist

A blacklist, of course, is the exact opposite of a whitelist. A blacklist can be used to strip HTML `<script>` tags or other non-conforming text from inputs before using input values. This technique suffers from the same shortcomings of the above section, Rejecting Bad Inputs on page 35. This type of sanitization must be done recursively until the value no longer changes. For example if the value `<scr`**`<script`**`ipt foo bar` is only processed once the result would be still contain `<script`, but if done recursively, the result would be `foo bar`.

Sanitize Input Using Escaping

Escaping input is one of the easiest and best ways to deal with free-form text. Essentially, instead of trying to determine the parts of the input that are safe (as with the above strategies), you assume the input is unsafe. There are a few different ways to encode strings depending on how the value is used:

HTML/XML Encoding

Example Input:
```
<img src onerror='alert("haxor")'>
```

Result:
```
&lt;img src onerror=&#39;alert(&quot;haxor&quot;)&#39;&gt;
```

HTML/XML Attribute Encoding

Example Input:
```
<div attr="" injectedAttr="a value here"><div attr="">
```

Result:
```
<div attr="&quot; injectedAttr&#61;&quot;a value
 here&quot;&gt;&lt;div attr=&quot;">
```

JSON Encoding

Example Input:
```
{"key": "", anotherKey": "anotherValue"}
```

Result:
```
{"key": "\", anotherKey\": \"anotherValue\""}
```

Base64 Encoding

Example Input:
```
any random string or binary data
```

Result:
```
YW55IHJhbmRvbSBzdHJpbmcgb3IgYmluYXJ5IGRhdGE=
```

There are ways to escape just about any format you need SQL, CSV, LDAP, etc.

Do Nothing

The last type of input validation is the no-op. Along with being the easiest to implement it is the most dangerous and most strongly discouraged! Almost every application takes input from an untrusted source. Not validating inputs puts your application and users at risk.

Common Attacks

The examples in this chapter have discussed ways to validate inputs but have only hinted at the type of attacks used when inputs are not properly sanitized. Let's look at those potential attacks, and how to prevent them, now.

SQL Injection Attacks

SQL injection is by far the most common form of data sanitization attack, and remains number one in the OWASP Top 10 *(https://www.owasp.org/images/7/72/ OWASP_Top_10-2017_%28en%29.pdf.pdf)* (a popular list of the most commonly found and exploited software vulnerabilities). It's held the number one spot for over 10 years now.

SQL injection occurs when an attacker is able to query or modify a database due to poor input sanitization. Other query injection attacks are similar, as most are typically a result of string concatenation. In the following example, a simple user query string is built with concatenation.

```
userId = getFromInput("userId");
sql = "SELECT * FROM Users WHERE UserId = " + userId;
```

If the `userId` were `jcoder` the SQL query would be `"SELECT * FROM Users WHERE UserId = jcoder`, however, a malicious attacker might input `jcoder; DROP TABLE ImportantStuff` which would result in two statements being executed:

```
SELECT * FROM Users WHERE UserId = jcoder;
DROP TABLE ImportantStuff
```

Similarly, the user could enter `jcoder OR 1=1` which would query for a user with the ID of `jcoder` OR `true` (`1=1` is always true), this would return all of the users in the system.

The cause of this issue is the use of poor string concatenation. In the example above, the value of the `userId` input crosses a trust boundary and ends up getting executed. The best way around this is to use SQL prepared statements. The syntax for using prepared statements varies from language to language but the gist is that the above query would become `SELECT * FROM Users WHERE UserId = ?`. The question mark would be replaced with the input value and be evaluated as a string instead of changing the query itself.

Most web frameworks and ORM libraries provide tools to protect against SQL injection attacks, be sure to look through your developer library documentation to ensure you're using these tools properly.

XSS - Cross Site Scripting

A cross-site scripting attack (XSS) is an attack that executes code in a web page viewed by a user. There are three different types of XSS attacks:

- **Stored XSS** - A persisted (in a database, log, etc) payload is rendered to an HTML page. For example, content on an forum.
- **Reflected XSS** - Attack payload is submitted by a user, the rendered server response contains the executed code. This differs from Stored XSS where as the attack payload is not persisted, but instead delivered as part of the request, eg. a

link: `http://example.com/`
`login?userId=<script>alert(document.cookie)</script>`
- **DOM based XSS** - The attack payload is executed as the result of an HTML page's DOM changing. With DOM based XSS the attack payload may not leave the victim's browser. The client side Javascript is exploited.

There are tons of resources online *(https://www.owasp.org/index.php/Cross-site_Scripting_%28XSS%29)* that cover this topic in great detail, so I'll only provide a basic example here. Earlier in this chapter the string `<img src onerror='alert("haxor")'>` was posted as a Reddit comment. If this string isn't correctly escaped it would have resulted in an annoying popup, shown in Figure 3-2.

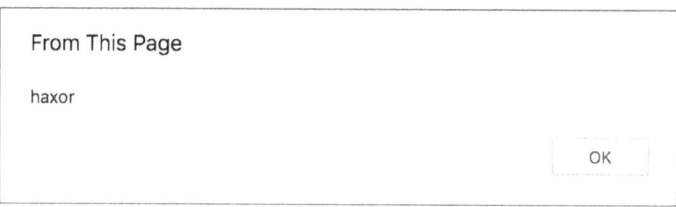

Figure 3-2: A JavaScript alert popup

You may see `alert()` used throughout examples when describing these attacks. The idea is if you can cause an alert to happen in the browser, you can execute other code that does something more malicious like sends your information (cookie, session ID, or other personal info) to a remote site.

File upload attacks

It is common for sites to support file uploads, particularly images such as profile avatars or photos. When uploading files, it is necessary to validate the type, size, and contents of these files. For example, if a user is uploading an avatar image, it's important to ensure the newly uploaded file is actually an image.

If an attacker can upload a PHP file named `avatar.php` instead of an image file, then later retrieve the file, unexpected and disastrous

Chapter 3: Sanitizing Data

behavior may occur. Imagine what would happen if that file is executed on the server, you could have a remote code exploit on your hands. There are a few things you can do to prevent this type of attack:

Validate expected file types Check that file size is reasonable (if someone is uploading a 1GB image, you might have a problem) If storing the file to disk, do NOT use a user input field as part of the file name, eg: `../../../etc/config.file` Always serve the files with the correct Content-Type header (image/png, audio/mpeg) Run a virus scan on all uploaded files Do not allow uploads of web executed files: php, cgi, js, swf, etc. Process the files - rename, resize, remove exif data, etc - before displaying back to the user

Look For Other Attack Vectors

Inputs are everywhere, often only evident in hindsight. User input and file uploads are just the tip of the iceberg, but what if we consider more than input and instead the code itself? Here are a couple of examples to illustrate this point.

Your Dependencies

Do you trust all of your dependencies? How about all of the transitive dependencies of your application? It is not uncommon to for an application to have a page that lists its dependencies versions and licenses (the later might even be required depending on the license). The popular Node package manager (npm) has had a few projects which have contained maliciously formed license fields *(https://blog.npmjs.org/post/80277229932/newly-paranoid-maintainers)*. In another npm incident, packages ran malicious scripts *(https://iamakulov.com/notes/npm-malicious-packages/)* upon installation automatically that uploaded the user's environment variables to a third party.

Every dependency is code you include from other systems across your trust boundary. Properly inspecting and validating your dependencies is a critical first step of any input sanitation plan. GitHub recently introduced automated security alerting *(https://blog.github.com/2017-11-16-introducing-security-alerts-on-github/)* to let you know when your dependencies might have security issues. Pay attention to these and you can prevent a lot of headaches.

Inbound HTML Requests

Almost all values from an HTTP request can be changed by the sender and need to be handled accordingly. To help illustrate this, here is a simple HTTP POST including numerous headers to `http://example.com/submit-me`:

```
POST /submit-me HTTP/1.1
Host: example.com
Accept: */*
Referer: http://example.com/fake.html
Accept-Language: en-us
Content-Type: application/x-www-form-urlencoded
Accept-Encoding: gzip, deflate
User-Agent: My Fake UserAgent <img src onerror='alert("haxor")'>
Content-Length: 37
Connection: Keep-Alive
Cache-Control: no-cache

foo=bar&key=value
```

You can see right away: request headers are user input too. Imagine for a moment that an HTTP client maliciously changes the User-Agent header. The logged User-Agent may falsely identify a request as coming from a different client application than the one in which it really originated.originated from. While that's unlikely to affect the current request, it might cause confusion in the application's logging and reporting system.

Further, the User-Agent could be visible from an internal web application that doesn't sanitize the User-Agent values before displaying them. In this case, an HTTP client could maliciously modify their User-Agent to any JavaScript code they want which would then be executed in an internal user's browser via XSS.

As these examples illustrate, even sanitizing relatively innocuous inputs is an important part of an overall security strategy.

Best Practices for Secure Data

While this chapter provides an overview of a few common types of attacks, there are many more out there.

First, you don't need to be an expert to prevent these attacks, but you do need to have some knowledge of them. The Open Web Application Security Project at *OWASP.org* is a great source information and examples on how to secure your application, often in multiple programming languages.

One of the most straightforward means of prevention is not to reinvent the wheel, and use an existing framework. Most frameworks contain tools to properly escape values, both on the frontend and backend, when used correctly.

Next, don't forget to monitor your application dependencies. There are mailing lists as well as open source and commercial tools to help you. New CVEs (Common Vulnerabilities and Exposures) are reported all of the time. For example, at the time of this writing a popular Java Web Container, Apache Tomcat 8, has about 60 CVEs *(https://tomcat.apache.org/security-8.html)* reported (and fixed). These reports, and the subsequent releases indicate that the project takes security seriously and updates regularly.

And finally, trust no one! As you have seen, any input into your API is an attack vector. Everything from an HTTP request to data returned from a database query to the files user upload could be dangerous. Proper data validation and sanitization goes a long way to help mitigate risk.

Chapter 4

Managing API Credentials

By Joël Franusic

A critical part of designing an API is determining how to grant users access to sensitive or important parts of it. While many APIs have publicly accessible endpoints that don't require authentication, the vast majority of APIs require a user to authenticate before any request can be fulfilled.

You need to authenticate with Stripe to charge a credit card, you have to authenticate with Twilio to send an SMS, and you have to authenticate with SendGrid to send an email. There's really no way to avoid authentication.

This chapter will cover two main aspects of managing API tokens:

- Protecting tokens that you use to connect to other APIs
- Advice and suggestions for what sort of API token to use for an API that you are building

Keep Your Credentials Private

No matter whether you are using an API or building your own, the advice applies to you: Never put an API secret into your code. Never ever!

The biggest problem with storing credentials in source code is that once a credential is in source code it's exposed to any developers who have access to that code, including your version control provider.

Many people use GitHub to host their source code — what happens when you push company code containing sensitive credentials? That means GitHub staff can now view your credentials; it's a security risk. If that project is later shared with contractors, partners, customers, or even made public, your secret is no longer secret. The same is true for open source projects — accidentally publishing test API tokens or other sensitive data will cause enormous problems. There are attackers who scan GitHub commits looking for sensitive data like Amazon Web Services API tokens and then use these credentials to do things like mine cryptocurrencies, form botnets, and enable fraud.

If you can't store your credentials in source code, how should you authenticate to your databases or 3rd party APIs? The short answer is to use environment variables instead. What that means is ignoring what you see in sample code (where secrets are entered directly into source) and instead loading secrets from environment variables which are managed from outside your source code and will not be stored in version control and every team member's text editor.

Below are two short snippets of sample code that demonstrate how important it is to use environment variables to store credentials.

Below we have some example Python code from Twilio. In this example, the `AC01a2bcd3e4fg567h89012i34jklmnop5` string is the "username" or "account ID" and the the `01234567890a12b34c567890de123fg4` string is the API token.

```
from twilio.rest import Client

account_sid = "AC01a2bcd3e4fg567h89012i34jklmnop5"
auth_token = "01234567890a12b34c567890de123fg4"
client = Client(account_sid, auth_token)
```

As you can see above, these API credentials are hard-coded into the program's source. This is a big no-no. Instead, as an example of what you *should* do, take a look at this example code from SendGrid, which uses the "os.environ.get" method in Python to grab the SendGrid API token from the SENDGRID_API_KEY environment variable.

```
import os
import sendgrid
from sendgrid.helpers.mail import *

apikey=os.environ.get('SENDGRID_API_KEY')
sg = sendgrid.SendGridAPIClient(apikey)
```

By pulling sensitive credentials from environment variables, which can be managed by configuration management and secret management software, your application code will remain credential-free.

Using environment variables to store secrets is an incredibly important first step to take in securing your code.

Choosing a Type of API Token

Now that we've covered general advice for storing and using API tokens, let's review common options for securing your API. We'll cover the different types of API tokens, touch on the advantages and disadvantages of each, and summarize with suggestions and a recommended approach.

Secure Your API

First, let's dig into some best practices:

- If your API is intended to be used to support an end user application, secure it using OAuth 2.0 to act as a Resource Server (RS) as defined by the OAuth 2.0 specification.
- If your API is intended to be used as a service by other

software, secure your API using an "API token" - a string that is unique for each client.

The first approach, implementing an OAuth 2.0 Resource Server, is intended to be used when an application is acting on behalf of the person using the app. The Instagram and Spotify APIs are great examples where every action of the API needs the user's context to make sense.

The second approach, using an API token, is the best approach for automated software. Stripe, Twilio, and SendGrid are examples of this type of an API. While you certainly can, and eventually should consider, implementing OAuth 2.0 access tokens, doing so may be more overhead than telling your users to just use an API token.

Regardless of approach, the following patterns apply:

- Use the `Authorization: Bearer` header for authenticating to your API. The single most important reason is that URL parameters are captured in server access logs and caches. Any "secret" included as a parameter is no longer a secret. As a standard defined by RFC 6750, most HTTP clients have built-in methods for using Bearer tokens.
- Further, instead of using a simple unique string, use a JSON Web Token or JWT as the Bearer token. By using JWT and the claims defined by RFC 7519, you can support a wide range of scenarios using just one authentication method. And, since JWT is such a widely adopted standard, most programming languages and frameworks have first-class JWT decoding and validation built in. You get more flexibility and wider compatibility with less work!

Another important thing to keep in mind is that by using a JWT as a Bearer token, you can support both token types that we describe above. A JWT works equally well as an OAuth 2.0 access token or as an "opaque" generic API token. You could start by just offering authenticating with an API token, but later add support for OAuth 2.0 and give your customers the features that OAuth 2.0 easily enables like automatic rotation of access tokens. You and your users get a clear, simple upgrade path for the life of your API.

Other Options for Authentication to Your API Service

Now, while I suggest that you have your clients authenticate to your API using JWTs as Bearer tokens, there are other patterns you will encounter. Below is a short list of other approaches to API authentication. Keep in mind that this is by no means an exhaustive list, just a list of the most common approaches and their tradeoffs:

Basic Authentication

This is the good 'ole "username and password" form of authentication method. Some APIs will use other words for "username" and "password" for example, Twilio calls the "username" the "Account SID" and the "password" the "Auth Token" but it works exactly the same.

If you decide to use Basic Auth to secure your API, keep in mind that your "username" and "password" should be random strings and not the same as the account username and password. You can generate these values by using an entropy source from your operating system (`/dev/random` on Unix-like systems or CryptGenRandom on Windows systems)

Opaque Tokens

These were the most common type of API token for APIs designed before OAuth 2.0 was standardized. Companies that use these types of token to secure their APIs include Stripe (with tokens that look like this: `sk_test_ABcdefGHiJkL0MnOpQ1rstU2`), and Okta (with tokens that look like this `00aBCdE0FGHijklmNO1pQ2RStuvWx34Y5z67ABCDEf`). These tokens have no relationship with the account information and mean absolutely nothing outside those systems.

As with basic auth strings, we suggest that you generate opaque tokens using an entropy source from your operating system.

Another best practice for opaque tokens is to allow multiple tokens to be issued and used at the same time, as this will allow for key rotation.

Signed or Hashed Tokens

These tokens are cryptographically signed or hashed and can either be opaque tokens or contain carry information about themselves. One reason to use a signed or hashed token is to allow your API to validate tokens without the need for a database lookup. The best supported token type in this category is the JWT used for OpenID Connect. Other examples of tokens in this category include PASETO and Hawk. In general, we suggest using JWTs as described above.

Advanced API Token Considerations

Using OAuth 2.0 with OIDC, or just a JWT as a Bearer token is a significant milestone in the ongoing task of keeping your API secure. Depending on use case, type of data, and type of operations your API provides, you may need to consider additional steps to secure your API. Keep in mind that these extra considerations might not be appropriate for every kind of API. If your API is a fan-made API that gives programmatic access to Star Wars data (like swapi.co), simple API keys are probably sufficient. However, if your API deals with things in the real world or any form of sensitive data, you should consider the options below and choose the combination appropriate for your API and fits your compliance requirements.

Implement API Token Rotation

A great next step to take in securing an API is to rotate the API token automatically. Like passwords, regularly changing an API token will limit the damage a leaked or misplaced API token can cause. More importantly, by considering and implementing this from the beginning, if a token is leaked or when an employee leaves the team, you have a process for quickly responding and protecting your systems.

Additionally, one of the great side-effects of frequent API token rotation is that it forces best security practices. Sometimes, when a team is in a rush to deliver a critical feature, corners get cut and hard coding an API token instead of storing it properly may save a few minutes in the short term. If you rotate tokens on a regular basis, developers have to follow the rules, otherwise their code will stop working on the next rotation.

If you are using OAuth 2.0 to secure your API, token rotation is built-in to the OAuth 2.0 standard: An "access_token" always has a limited lifespan and must be rotated periodically using the "refresh_token". As an additional benefit, if you're using an OAuth server such as Okta, when you exchange the refresh_token for a new access_token, your authorization policies are re-evaluated. If a user's API access has been limited, increased, or even revoked, your application will know.

Outside of OAuth 2.0, there isn't an accepted best practice for implementing token rotation. Therefore your best and easiest option is to implement OAuth 2.0. Once you have a system in place to manage your API tokens, it makes sense to start rotating API tokens on a regular basis. Your specific rotation schedule will depend on the use case. For read/write operations in banking or healthcare, rotating every 5 or 10 minutes might be necessary. For read only access to a public Twitter feed, annually is probably sufficient. Regardless, you should always rotate keys after an employee leaves the team to protect against accidental or intentional misuse of API tokens by former employees.

Ideally, key rotation should also be paired with configuring your API to log events into a "Security and Information and Event Management" (SIEM) system that you can use to monitor your API for suspicious events.

Monitor for Token Leaks

In addition to the use of SIEM systems as suggested above, an advanced technique is to scan sites like GitHub and S3 for leaked API keys. No best practices have emerged in this area yet, but a good technique should include automatically disabling and notifying end users when a token has been discovered in public as part of a scan.

Quite a few open source projects can be found that will scan for leaked tokens, a good way to find these services is to search for "github credential scan"

Bind Tokens to TLS Sessions

Finally, an interesting emerging technique that I'm keeping my eye on is the binding of tokens to TLS sessions. This technique is described in RFC 5056 *(https://tools.ietf.org/html/rfc5056)* and RFC 5929 *(https://tools.ietf.org/html/rfc5929).*

The basic idea with "channel binding" is to tie an API token to a specific TLS session. In practice this would mean writing your API to issue tokens that can only be used in the same TLS session. This way, if an API token is compromised from a client, an attacker can't move that token to another client or machine because they would have a different TLS session for the initial issuer. This still isn't foolproof but the work and effort for the attacker just multiplied.

Key Takeaways for Managing API Credentials

In closing, here is my best advice for managing API credentials:

- Never paste a secret into your code. Never ever!
- Secure your API using OAuth 2.0 by writing your API to act as an OAuth 2.0 "Resource Server"
- Use JSON Web Tokens (JWT) as your tokens to embed additional context
- Use the token as a Bearer token with the Authorization header to prevent leaking your token in logs and caches
- Implement regular token rotation to reduce the damage from leaked keys, poor practices, honest mistakes, and disgruntled employees.
- Monitor your source code for token leaks
- Implement "channel binding" to tie your API tokens to the TLS session they are requested over

Chapter 5

Authentication

By Matt Raible

Authentication is the process of proving who you are. In the real world, you authenticate every day. You show your driver's license when you use your credit card, you show your passport when you embark on an international flight, and you show your driver's license when you get pulled over by a police officer. In the real world, the driver's license and passport serve as proof of your identity.

On the internet, you're accustomed to proving who you are by typing in a username and password. In this way, your credentials are like your driver's license. They verify you.

APIs are different from web applications in that they rarely have a *face*. They're often just buckets of data that get their information exposed via API calls, also known as HTTP requests. APIs are for programmers and applications; they're rarely exposed to end users. As a result, programmers have more but options for authentication but they all have tradeoffs.

HTTP-based APIs are the most common, so let's begin by talking about some options built into the protocol.

Note: All authentication options described in this chapter **must** all happen over an HTTPS (TLS) connection to be secure.

API Authentication Options

The first type of API authentication I'll talk about is HTTP Basic Authentication.

HTTP Basic Authentication is defined by RFC 7617 *(https://tools.ietf.org/html/rfc7617)*. This document was created in September 2015 by the internet standards body known as The Internet Engineering Task Force (IETF). It replaces RFC 2617 *(https://tools.ietf.org/html/rfc2617)*, which was created in 1999 and defined both basic and digest authentication.

Basic authentication is the simplest form of web authentication. It's a stateless protocol that doesn't require cookies, session identifiers, or login pages (like most other forms of web authentication today).

HTTP Basic Authentication

Basic authentication works as follows:

1. When a client sends a request to the server, the server returns a 401 Unauthorized response status and provides information on how to authenticate with a www-Authenticate response header.
2. If the client is a browser, a built-in browser dialog will prompt the user for a username and password. A programmer has no control over what this dialog looks like.
3. When a browser sends the user's credentials to the server, the username and password are combined with a colon separator (username:password), base64-encoded, then added to the Authorization header like so:

```
Authorization: Basic base64(username:password)
```

The server will receive this request, decode the authorization header, split on the colon, and use the credentials to validate the user has access to perform the operation.

When using HTTP Basic Authentication to secure APIs, its recommended the username and password be long, random strings rather than easy-to-remember names. Entropy means a "lack of order and predictability" and is very important for passwords, especially if you're generating them. The more random your password generation process is, the better. One important aspect is that the API username and password must not be the same username and password as the account's username and password. Not only are their security implications of using the same credentials but something as simple as clicking "forgot password" can knock your applications offline.

While basic auth is perfectly fine to use, one of its issues is that your username+password are sent over the network on every request. This increases the likelihood that they could be leaked, logged, or reused in other applications.

Basic authentication has other long term issues as well:

- **Key rotation** - What happens if you have an app running with basic authentication in production and you accidentally publish your API key on GitHub? As an API provider, you need a strategy for supporting multiple keys so your users can rotate them without downtime.
- **Delegation** - If you're building an API that needs to run for a third party (like a Google API for grabbing someone's friends), you don't want to use Basic because it would require a username/password to be given to your app from a user. If this is the account username, there is no delegation or scoping of permissions.
- **Browsers** - If your API needs to be consumed from an insecure environment (JavaScript front end, mobile app, etc.), you can't just embed an API key in your app, otherwise attackers would grab it and do bad things.

Several authentication schemes use the HTTP authentication framework. Schemes can differ in security strength and their availability in client or server software. All schemes use an Authorization header followed by scheme name and a space character. Common scheme names *(https://developer.mozilla.org/ en-US/docs/Web/HTTP/Authentication#Authentication_schemes)* include:

- Basic
- Digest
- Bearer (for OAuth 2.0)
- HOBA (HTTP Origin-Bound Authentication, RFC 7486, draft)
- Mutual (Mutual Authentication Protocol, draft)
- Signature (HTTP Signatures and AWS4-HMAC-SHA256)

Basic authentication is easy to implement for APIs, but it's not often used in web applications because the login form can't be customized and "logging out" requires closing the browser.

Federated Identity

Federated identity is a way to use an account from one website to create an account and log in to a different site.

There are two main players in a federated identity system: an Identity Provider (IdP) and a Service Provider (SP). Often, the service provider is the application that you need to log in to, and the IdP is the provider of the users that can log in.

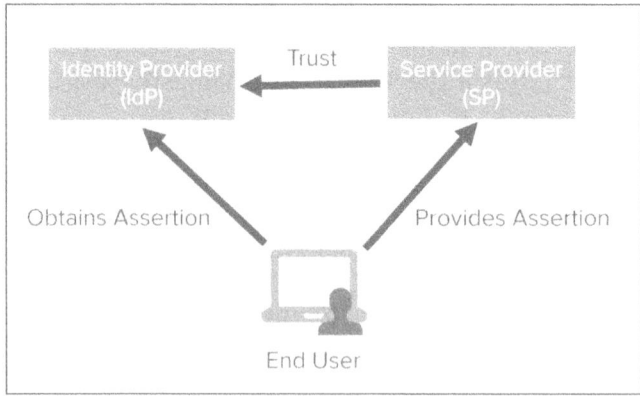

Figure 5-1: Federated Identity

OAuth 2.0

OAuth 2.0 is a delegated authorization framework which is ideal for APIs. It enables apps to obtain limited access (scopes) to a user's data without giving away a user's password. It decouples authentication from authorization and supports multiple use cases addressing different device capabilities. It supports server-to-server apps, browser-based apps, mobile/native apps, and consoles/TVs.

OAuth is like a hotel key card, but for apps. If you have a hotel key card, you can get access to your room, the business center, and potentially the gym. How do you get a hotel key card? You have to do an authentication process at the front desk to get it. After authenticating and obtaining the keycard, you can only access the places and things the hotel has authorized you to use.

It's worth remembering that although there are two things called OAuth - OAuth 1.0a (RFC 5849) and OAuth 2.0 (RFC 6749) - these specifications are completely different from one another and cannot be used together; there is no backward compatibility between them. Whenever we say OAuth here, assume we mean OAuth 2.0.

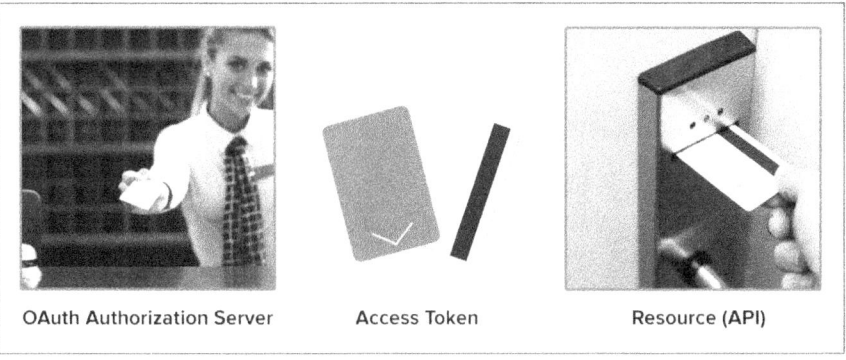

OAuth Authorization Server   Access Token   Resource (API)

Figure 5-2: OAuth is like a hotel key card, but for apps!

To break it down simply, OAuth is where:

1. App requests authorization from User
2. User authorizes App and delivers proof of authorization

3. App presents proof of authorization to the authorization server to get a Token
4. The Token is restricted to only access what the User authorized for the specific App
5. Resources (APIs) validate the Token as having the proper and expected authorizations

Client applications can be public or confidential. There is a significant distinction between the two in OAuth nomenclature. Confidential clients can be trusted to store a secret because they have backend storage unavailable to review or attack. They're not running on a desktop or distributed through an app store. People can't reverse engineer them and get the secret key. They're running in a protected area where end users can't access them.

Public clients are browsers, mobile apps, and IoT devices. The code on these devices can be extracted, decompiled, and reviewed. Therefore, we can't store any sensitive information in the application itself and expect it to be protected. Do not embed a password or secret information - including URLs - of any form in these types of applications!

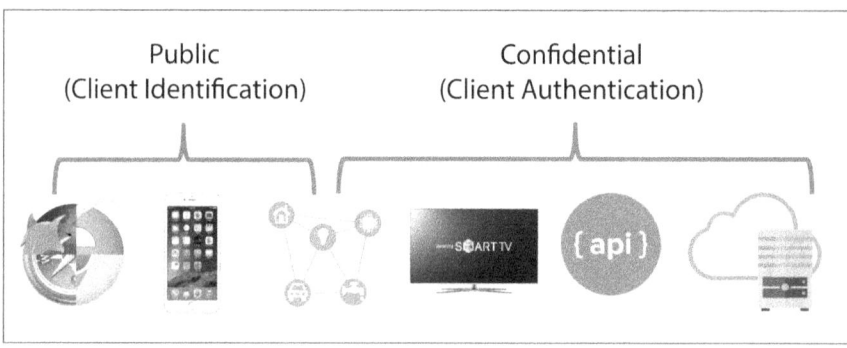

Figure 5-3: Public vs confidential clients

The core OAuth specification describes two types of tokens: an access token and a refresh token. The client uses the access token to access an API (aka Resource Server). They're meant to be short-lived and work over a span of minutes or hours, not days or months. Due to this, the core OAuth specification doesn't have an approach to

Chapter 5: Authentication

revoking access tokens but in many cases you will need to as a token could have been compromised or a subscription has expired. To address that RFC 7009 *(https://tools.ietf.org/html/rfc7009)* describes an additional endpoint to revoke a token. To be specific, this revokes it with the Authorization Server, not the Resource Server (API). Unless the Resource Server checks with the Authorization Server, it will not know the token has been revoked. This happens in the real world where you could still use your driver license to board a flight, even if it has been revoked.

The other token is the refresh token. This is much longer-lived and may last for days, months, or years. This token is used exclusively to get a new access token. Because a refresh token effectively persists access long term, getting them requires a confidential clients and they can be revoked more easily.

Next, the OAuth spec doesn't define how a token is structured, its contents, or how it's encoded. It can be anything you want but generally you'll want a JSON Web Token (JWT) as defined by RFC 7519 *(https://tools.ietf.org/html/rfc7519)* In a nutshell, a JWT (pronounced "jot") is a secure and trustworthy standard for token authentication. JWTs allow you to digitally sign information (referred to as claims) with a signature and can be verified at a later time with a public/private key pair.

Tokens are retrieved from endpoints on an authorization server. The two main endpoints are the authorization endpoint and the token endpoint. They're separated for different use cases.

The authorization endpoint is where the app goes to get authorization and consent from the user. This returns an authorization code that says the user has consented to the app's request. Then the authorization code is passed to the token endpoint which processes the request and says "great, here's your access token and your refresh token."

Now you use the access token to make requests to the API. Once it expires, you use the refresh token with the token endpoint to get a new access and refresh tokens.

Because these tokens can be short-lived and scale out, they can't be revoked; you have to wait for them to time out.

OAuth uses two channels: a front channel and a back channel. The front channel is what goes over the browser. The back channel is a secure HTTP call directly from the client application to the resource server, such as the request to exchange the authorization code for tokens. These channels are used for different flows depending on what device capabilities you have.

To address the differences between web apps, mobile clients, IoT devices, and even other APIs, there are numerous OAuth grant types or flows. The first four are defined in the core specification while the other three come from extensions.

1. **Implicit Flow** - everything happens in the browser, on the front channel. Common in single page applications (SPAs).
2. **Authorization Code Flow** - the front channel is used to get an authorization code. The back channel is used by the client application to exchange the authorization code for an access token (and optionally a refresh token). This is the gold standard of OAuth flows.
3. **Client Credentials Flow** - often used for server-to-server and service account scenarios. It's a back channel only flow to obtain an access token using the client's credentials. It differs from most of the other flows in that there is no user involved.
4. **Resource Owner Password Flow** - a legacy flow that allows you to pass a username and password to the authorization server. Only recommended when you have old-school clients to accommodate.
5. **Assertion Flow** - similar to the Client Credentials flow. This was added to open up the idea of federation. This flow allows an Authorization Server to trust authorization grants from third parties such as SAML IdP. The Authorization Server trusts the Identity Provider. This is described further in RFC 7521 *(https://tools.ietf.org/html/rfc7521)*.
6. **Device Flow** - often used with TVs, command line interfaces, and other devices without a web browser or with limited

input options. The device first obtains a short "user code" from the authorization server, and the device prompts the user to enter that code on a separate device such as their mobile phone or computer. The client polls the authorization server via a back channel an access token, and optionally a refresh token is returned after the user authorizes the request. This is described further in the OAuth Device Flow draft spec *(https://tools.ietf.org/html/draft-ietf-oauth-device-flow)*.

7. **Authorization Code Flow** + PKCE - the recommended flow for native apps on mobile devices. In this flow, the native app sends a PKCE code challenge along with the authentication request. This is described further in what's commonly known as the "AppAuth spec *(https://tools.ietf.org/html/draft-ietf-oauth-native-apps-12)*".

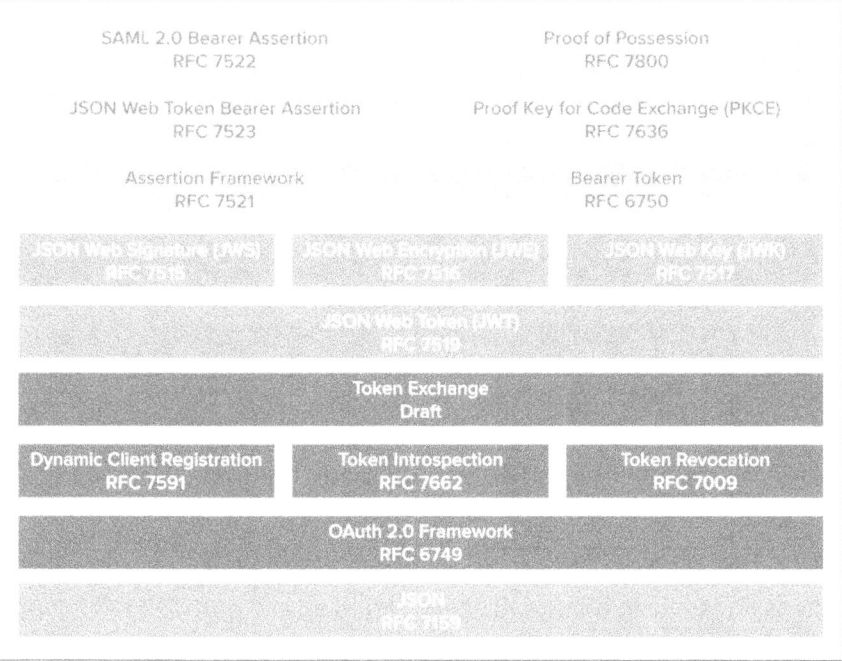

Figure 5-4: Authorization Framework: Return of complexity through extensions

There's a huge number of additions that happened to OAuth in the last several years. These add complexity back on top of OAuth to complete a variety of enterprise scenarios. In Figure 5-4, you can see how JSON and OAuth are the foundation. JWT, JWK, JWE, and JWS can be used as interoperable tokens that can be signed and encrypted.

Common Misconceptions about OAuth 2.0

OAuth 2.0 is not an authentication protocol. It explicitly says so in its documentation *(https://oauth.net/articles/authentication/)*.

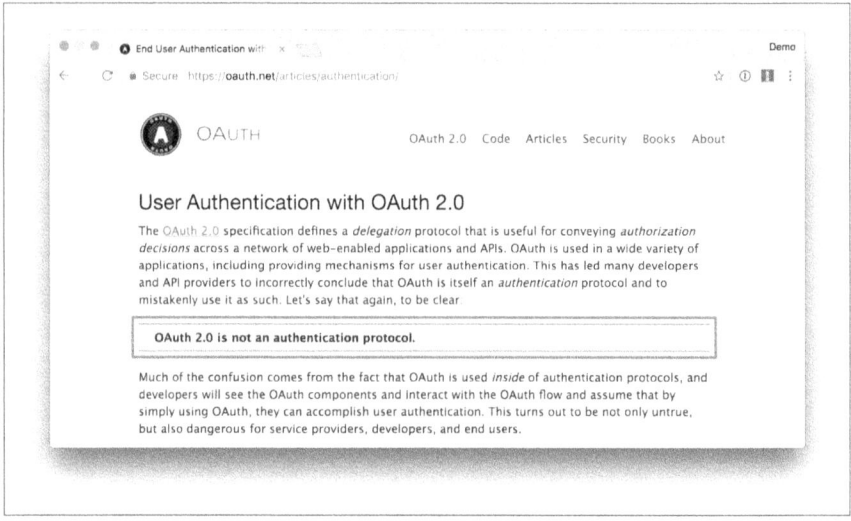

Figure 5-5: OAuth is not an authentication protocol (oauth.net)

While it's easy to lose that distinction, note that everything so far has been about delegated authorization. OAuth 2.0 alone says absolutely nothing about the user such as how they authenticate or what information we have about them. We simply have a token to access a resource. Pseudo-Authentication with OAuth 2.0 Login with OAuth was made famous by Facebook Connect and Twitter. In this flow, a client accesses a /me endpoint with an access token. People invented this endpoint as a way of getting back a user profile with an access token. It's a non-standard way to get information about the user. There's no specification to support this and in fact, it was a originally a misuse of the standard networks. Access tokens are meant to be opaque. They're meant for the API; they're not designed to contain user information.

What you're really trying to answer with authentication is *who* the user is, *when* did the user authenticate, and *how* did the user authenticate. You can answer typically answer these questions with SAML assertions, not with access tokens and authorization grants. That's why it's called this pseudo authentication.

OpenID Connect (OIDC)

To solve the pseudo authentication problem, a number of social and identity providers combined best parts of OAuth 2.0, Facebook Connect, and SAML 2.0 to create OpenID Connect *(http://openid.net/connect/)* or OIDC.

Once again, despite the very similar name, OpenID Connect is not based on or compatible with the original OpenID specification. The name comes from the OpenID Foundation which promotes, protects, and nurtures the technologies and communities involved in identity on the web.

At a technical level, OIDC extends OAuth 2.0 with a new token called the id_token on the client application side and the UserInfo endpoint on the server side. They both benefit from having a specific, limited set of scopes and well-defined set of user-related claims. By combining them, an application can request information on a user's profile, email, address, and even phone number in a consistent way regardless of the OIDC provider.

OIDC was made famous by Google, Facebook, and Microsoft, all big early adopters. The single most important part is that the consistent scopes and claims make implementations fast, easier, and compatible regardless of the provider.

Generally, an OpenID Connect flow involves the following steps:

1. Discover OIDC metadata as defined in the specification *(http://openid.net/specs/openid-connect-discovery-1_0.html)*
2. Perform the OAuth flow to obtain id token and access token
3. Validate JWT ID token locally based on built-in dates and signature
4. Get additional user attributes as needed with the access token at the UserInfo endpoint

In terms of implementation, an ID token is a JSON Web Token (JWT) which adheres to the specification and is small enough to pass between devices

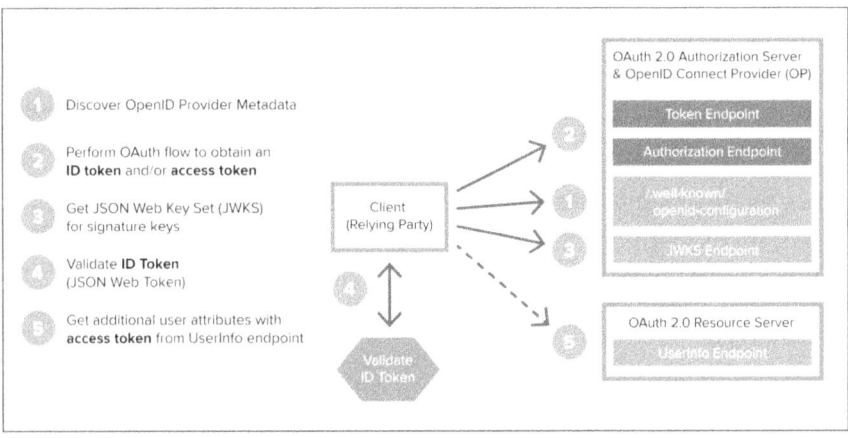

Figure 5-6: OpenID Connect Flow

The Authorization Code Flow can also be used with Native apps. In this scenario, the native app sends a PKCE code challenge along with the authentication request. PKCE (pronounced "pixy") stands for Proof Key for Code Exchange and is defined by RFC 7636 *(https://tools.ietf.org/html/rfc7636)*.

OIDC is an excellent addition to and special case of OAuth because it allows you to get a user's information and learn more about them.

Recommended Best Practices for Authentication

Using industry standard authentication protocols will help you secure your API in well-understood, predictable, and scalable ways that allow your team to use established services, components, and libraries while not confusing end users.

If you're building an API for server-side clients, you essentially have three choices when implementing authentication:

HTTP Basic Authentication: This is the simplest option, but doesn't provide the security and key rotation benefits of OAuth Client Credentials.

Digest Authentication: This is what many large providers use with various customizations, most famously, Amazon. Unless you have a very pressing security need, I recommend you not use Digest Authentication as it requires a lot of engineering work to implement and maintain, and shifts the security burden to you.

OAuth Client Credentials: This is the only OAuth flow designed for server-side clients to use. The client will exchange their ID and secret for a token. If you're building an API and want to reduce security risk over the network, using OAuth Client Credentials is a good option.

If you're building an API for a mobile client, you should always use the OIDC Authorization Code flow with PKCE (as explained in the OpenID Connect section above).

If you're building an API for a web app with a server-side backend, you should always use the OIDC Authorization Code flow.

If you're building an API for single-page app (e.g. a React app) that has no server-side backend, then the only type of authentication you can use is the OIDC Implicit flow as described earlier.

By following these guidelines and using the correct form of authentication for the correct type of API, you can feel confident in your implementation and give your users a sense of security, regardless of what type of app client is being used.

Chapter 6

Authorization

By Sai Maddali

In the previous chapter we discussed authentication and the various ways of authenticating an entity. We learned that authentication *only* deals with validating the identity of an entity. It answers "Who are you?" Thus, authentication doesn't answer "What are you allowed to do?" That's the realm of authorization. Once an entity is authenticated into a system, that system needs to understand whether the authenticated entity can access, view, or interact with something.

Let's consider an example. When you log into your bank account, you're considered authenticated – but that doesn't mean you're necessarily authorized to perform certain actions, like withdrawing funds. Just being logged in doesn't also allow you to withdraw $1,000,000. This is why when you buy something at the store with your credit card, the card reader says "Authorizing" and not "Authenticating." It's trying to verify whether you have enough funds in your account to make a purchase.

In this chapter I'll give you a brief overview of the various types of authorization and how they can be utilized to your advantage when building API services.

Types of Authorization

While each authorization type has its pros/cons, the goal is to convey when to use one scheme over the other. We will cover hierarchical, role-based, attribute-based, and delegated authorization.

Hierarchical

Hierarchical authorization is exactly what it sounds like — authorization determined based on the hierarchy. As you might imagine, within this structure permissions are determined by an entity's place in the hierarchy.

One good example of this is organizational hierarchy. Imagine Wookie Inc. is a social music streaming service specifically for hip hop listeners. Beyond music streaming, it also has its own publishing business that discovers new artists and manages them.

It has the following divisions: Marketing, Talent Management, Engineering, and Services. All of these main divisions have the following sub-divisions:

- Marketing has product, corporate, and partner marketing
- Talent Management has recruiting, contracts, and communications
- Engineering has infrastructure, QA, devops, and core engineering
- Services has support, customer success, and professional services.

In this hierarchical authorization model, the leader of the infrastructure engineering sub-division, should have access and view into everything in that infrastructure org but not necessarily the other sub-orgs like QA/devops and vice versa. Similarly, if we go a level above, the CTO leading the engineering org should have access to that entire org which includes all the sub orgs only in Engineering. Rinse and repeat.

Although it sounds simple, modelling authorization with a hierarchy is not an efficient model unless your app is really simple with barely any authorization decisions to make. Making authorization decisions in this model require expensive recursive database lookups. The most common queries – such as "is this employee in this group?" – require exploring a significant portion of the organization structure and the problem only gets worse as the organization grows.

Essentially, hierarchy is just an organizational chart, not a workable authorization model. It's important to think of hierarchical authorization that way because it's rarely a scalable or complete solution. Every system needs to understand the different roles that can use that system and everything that they are allowed to do within that system.

Role-Based Access Control

Many organizations have roles and responsibilities that don't quite fit a strict hierarchical structure. For example, a release manager on a development team may have access to deploy their components but their direct supervisor may not. Let's take a look at role-based access control, starting with a simple use case: one user creating another user.

Before we dig into implementation, there are a few questions to consider:

- Who can create the user?
- Where in the hierarchy can the user be?
- What user type can the user be?
- What permissions can the new user have?
- How do I model those permissions?

There are multiple ways this problem can be solved. We can pick a single user or group of users and only give them the permissions to create users and do other administrative tasks. But this is not a scalable approach. We need to have a more generic model for user-types and permissions. There are various approaches to tackle this but we will focus specifically on role-based access control or RBAC and attribute-based access control or ABAC.

To solve this problem, our hypothetical company, Wookie Inc., hires their first IT person, Han. He'll take care of all IT-related tasks. Because Han is an IT admin, he has the rights and privileges to create other users, delete them, and assign them to the right org/department. As usual, IT admin is the role type and the privileges are the permissions.

Similarly, engineering has Jr/Sr engineers, architects, development managers, and product managers and they all have different privileges. Junior engineers rarely have permission to touch production systems. Architects may have access to specific instances in AWS. Dev managers can change the status of ticket on JIRA. Similar responsibility boundaries and policies exist in every group of every organization.

The roles in an RBAC model are the de facto way of determining what permissions a user or service has. The great thing about RBAC is it enables you to apply both broad and granular access policies. You can use various objects like groups and scopes to make implementation easier.

You define different roles, what those roles can do, and assume some combination of them to users and you're done!

RBAC not only gives great control over how to manage access but is also a great model for auditing access. Once we create a consistent management framework it becomes easier to answer the question: "who has access to what?" RBAC creates a logical model that reflects the structure of system and its responsibilities.

Unfortunately, RBAC still has drawbacks. Imagine a company with 100k employees and thousands of roles with specific permissions or a microservices architecture with thousands of services, each needing fine-grained access to features and functionality of other microservices. Thousands of services each of which has its own unique set of permissions for how and when they can interact with each other. Building for these scenarios with RBAC introduces a lot of complexity:

- The number of roles will explode making management a nightmare.
- The scale makes it hard to validate and audit access. Nothing can stop me from accidentally assigning a user or service to the wrong group giving them wrong privileges.
- To handle this scale, roles become more generic and apply to many users or many services.

And it still doesn't address user specific data.

For example, let's say I am building a banking application. Only bankers who are temporarily authorized by the customer can carry out certain actions for that customer. How can this be enforced in my API? The banker role is generic but the authorization is user specific. The approval condition can be modelled as a user attribute and map to specific actions. These actions could be anything from withdrawing, reading balances, adding account admins, etc.

Attribute-Based Access Control

The pattern must be obvious by now – in ABAC, access is defined by the attributes on the user or service, and a policy that enforces what actions these attributes are allowed to perform. As we saw in the above section, implementing RBAC is relatively simple but maintaining it over time becomes cumbersome as the system grows and permissions get more fine-grained. With ABAC, it's the opposite. Implementing it can be a herculean task but once complete, maintaining it is relatively simple and efficient.

With RBAC, every action that can be carried out in a system is tied to a complex set of role combinations. If a new role is introduced, every action that this new role can access must be updated. However with ABAC, you can create a central policy engine in which you define complex boolean logic for what attributes are allowed to do based on various conditions. ABAC is a great model for fine-grained (deep/specific) access control whereas RBAC is good for coarse-grained (broad/generic) access control.

It's also important to note that attributes can be about anything or anyone:

- There can be user or subject attributes like name, ID, role, department, status
- There can be attributes to actions like CRUD: add, edit, remove, approve
- There can be resource attributes like the bank example we covered earlier: bank account, bank balance, or resource clarification like top secret, public access
- There can also be attributes about the context of an interaction: time, location, device

Let's revisit the Wookie Inc. example from the RBAC section. We created a simple RBAC management model for an IT admin As the organization grows and enters new markets, the access requirements also go up, introducing all sorts of complexity:

- HIPAA regulations specify only HIPAA certified users can look at user data
- To handle scale, Wookie Inc. decides to move to a microservices architecture
- Other compliance requirements mean that Wookie Inc. has to have a way to audit everything, including APIs.
- They have decided to open up some of their APIs for public access.

All of these requirements aren't uncommon for companies to address as they grow. Let's take a deeper look at the last one on the list: exposing APIs for public consumption. This can be third party developers that want to build against the platform or customers that need to build custom workflows. Either way, making sure the right user has the right privileges is incredibly important and difficult to implement. Unlike a product where actions are simple and what a user can do is based on roles, API actions are more granular.

This adds more complexity to API authorization Take a simple music playlist API, can the consumers of my API:

- Read what songs are in a users playlist?
- Add or delete songs from a playlist?
- Change the description?
- Change the playlist order? Sort it?

Even in the simplest of scenarios, authorization can get complex quickly.

All of these actions can be modelled as attributes of the resource that's being accessed. For example, being able to add, edit user details are attributes of the user resource. When writing code, I need a better way to model these attributes. We can utilize scopes here. If you recall, back in the Authentication chapter, OAuth 2.0 had the concept of scopes. We can use that model again here:

- User scopes: read:name, edit:name, read:email, edit:email
- Playlist scopes: read:playlist, edit:playlist, edit:description, sort:playlist

The naming convention can be anything you prefer. You could also model some of these as read_name, edit_name, etc.

We now have a model for all the resource types and the various actions that can be carried out on these resources. You can also take this a step further and define more granular attributes: playlists can be public or private. Songs can be explicit or non-explicit.

We can repeat the same model for users also. Users can:

- Be Account admins
- Be in listen only mode
- Be paid subscribers
- Be the primary account holder
- Have genre preferences.

These attributes can be defined on the user object however you like:

```
/users
    id
    Name
    admin
        yes or no
    subscription
        free, family, premium
    /preferences
    /profile
    /playlists
```

These are all user attributes and I can model the actions on them using scopes in a similar fashion:

- `read:account_status, edit:listening_mode, edit:genre_preferences`
- `edit:subscription, read:subscription, read:genre_preferences`

At the same time, you can use these user attributes to enforce access:

- Access to social groups in Wookie Inc. can be enforced based on genre preferences or subscription status
- Allowing users to skip songs and that can be based on their mode and subscription status

Using this model, you can now architect a simple model for making authorization decisions. ABAC has a standardized architecture that we can use. Let's take an simple example: Leia is a free user that wants to edit Han's workout playlist. Editing playlists depends on a simple factor: It is only available to paid members.

How would this flow?

There are multiple ways to architect this but ABAC proposes the following architecture:

- Policy Enforcement Point (PEP) - Think of this as a gateway. Its protecting all the resources and all requests are routed to this point to make a decision. It takes the incoming HTTP request and creates an authorization specific request.

- Policy Decision Point (PDP) - This is really the brain of the architecture. It consumes the authorization request sent from PEP, breaks it down, and evaluates all the attributes: Who is accessing? What attributes do they have? What are they requesting? With all this data in hand, it can consult various sources like a database or a 3rd party system like Okta or LDAP to make a decision.

Using this, let's see how Leia's request to edit Han's playlist will be evaluated:

Leia presses the "Edit Playlist" Button → Request is routed to PEP → PEP constructs an authorization request → PEP requests edi:playlist, edit:description scopes along with some identifying information like user id → PDP uses this information to lookup policy, user info, and returns allow or deny.

While this is a simple example, from it we can extrapolate more complex requests and apply the same architecture for an entire system. For APIs, the PEP is usually the API Gateway. This gateway can then rely on an internal policy engine or potentially using information from a 3rd party identity provider to act as the PDP.

ABAC is a powerful and flexible approach for API authorization that requires an early investment but scales efficiently as your requirements and use cases As a general rule of thumb to decide if ABAC is better than RBAC, estimate how granular your authorization must be. Starting with RBAC for a limited set of roles and actions is a safe choice but as the number of roles and permissions increase, ABAC becomes a better choice. ABAC is also great at establishing governance policies and implementing legal/ data protection compliance requirements.

The OAuth 2.0 framework is specifically designed for ABAC that works for many use cases, especially for APIs. When you combine it with tools like JWTs and OpenID Connect, you have a token which represents an authenticated user, additional context information such as their profile, and the scopes to which they have authorization. The OAuth 2.0 extensions allow you to implement RBAC + ABAC and scale as your API and use cases grow.

Key Takeaways

In closing, here's some simple advice on how to think about authorization in your APIs:

- Estimate the scopes or permissions required for your users to accomplish the use cases your API addresses early on
- Keep things simple. Don't overwhelm yourself or your app with unnecessary overhead. Most applications don't have complex authorization needs
- Building authorization is hard. For simple scenarios with a few user types and authorization decisions, your impulse will be to build it yourself. Unfortunately, requirements and policies almost always get more complex so this becomes less sustainable over time. Use a third-party authorization service, like Okta, whenever possible
- Even with a third party provider in place, it's still important to understand authorization so you can make good decisions on how to architect your application
- RBAC is enough for many use cases. ABAC is the next step
- OAuth 2.0 is an authorization framework that you can leverage for most scenarios
- Log everything. Authorization decisions must be reviewed and adjusted based on new use cases, usage patterns, and bad actors. Auditing becomes more important as you grow

Chapter 7
API Gateways

By Keith Casey

An API gateway is a firewall that sits between your API and your users. They range from the simplest proxies which apply throttling and white/blacklisting to fully configurable platforms with fine-grained access mapping individual permissions to specific HTTP verbs and endpoints. Realistically, using an API gateway is not necessary but it makes some things faster, easier, and more reliable, which allows you to focus on your API.

The most prominent gateways are Google's Apigee *(https://apigee.com/api-management/)*, Salesforce's MuleSoft *(https://www.mulesoft.com/)*, the AWS API Gateway *(https://aws.amazon.com/api-gateway/)*, Microsoft Azure's API Management *(https://azure.microsoft.com/en-us/services/api-management/)*, and the Kong API Gateway *(https://konghq.com/)* but the most appropriate gateway for your project will vary depending on context, use cases, and budget.

This section does not make a recommendation for a particular gateway but describes the process and use cases where one may fit.

Most API gateway vendors call themselves API management platforms because gateways are just one part of an overarching API management strategy. With that in mind, there are five key things that most API management platforms provide: Lifecycle management, interface management, access management, consumption tracking, and business goals.

When you're building and deploying your API, you need to address each of these five areas, which is one of the main reasons API management platforms have taken off in recent years: they make solving these problems tangibly easier.

The Role of an API Management Platform

Lifecycle Management

Effective API management begins long before your first HTTP request. In fact, it likely begins in a document or at a whiteboard with a simple requirement and business needs. It quickly turns into a specification and then a workflow and then a data and interaction model. Eventually, it probably turns into an Open API specification, deployable code, and metrics that are carefully tracked by the team.

The key technical aspect of this entire process is understanding what stage the API is in, how and where it's deployed, and how it's maintained. As a result, many of the gateways integrate with the cloud hosting services blend directly into your devops processes. Further, the process and these integrations are the same whether the APIs are destined for internal, partner, or even consumer use. In this area, that distinction is irrelevant.

Interface Management

While it's pedantic to note, the "I" in API stands for Interface, and it's the only interface our users will ever interact with. A full discussion of API design is beyond the scope of this book, but the result will always be individual URLs or endpoints we need to support, which HTTP verbs are applied and how, and what parameters or properties are required for each.

API management platforms do not help you choose specific endpoints or which verb is best. Instead, once you've made those decisions, the API gateway will allow you to map external URLs to specific endpoints in your API and whitelist specific HTTP verbs, parameters, and even datatypes each endpoint supports. As the first line of defense, this is one of the subtly powerful aspects of a gateway because it limits the surface area where your API can be attacked. That said, all the standard data sanitization practices still apply.

More advanced API management platforms go a step further. Instead of merely configuring the available endpoints via a web interface or even an API, you can upload your API specification document - like Open API, Blueprint, or RAML - and the gateway will parse the document and configure the external interface. You may even be able to integrate this with your continuous integration system to automatically deploy your API into staging, perform the appropriate checks, and prepare to deploy to production.

Access Management

Access management in an API management platform is where things begin to get more complex. Until this point, the platform has dealt with deeply technical challenges the solutions to which are expressed entirely in code. Access management - both authentication and authorization - is a combination of code, the context of the user and their use case, and business policies and practices. This makes it fundamentally more complicated.

At the simplest level, every gateway can use an API key that is checked on every request. While this works, it lacks the fine-grained access most security and compliance teams require.

As an alternative, many API gateways also include a basic OAuth 2.0 server. Your users perform a simple OAuth user flow, receive an access token, and can then use the API. There are two significant drawbacks to this approach. First, the gateway has to keep its own list of users and activate or deactivate them as employees come and go. As yet another independent system, it's easy for this information to get out of sync. The second drawback is that security teams can't review, audit, and validate the security policies implemented by the gateway. For some organizations, this is troubling at best and catastrophic at worst.

The final approach gateways take is to provide a pluggable interface for an external Identity Provider (IdP). Using an IdP is an easy way to integrate user management with a more extensive system such as Active Directory or Okta's Universal Directory. The single biggest benefit is simplicity: users are activated or deactivated in the API gateway as they are activated or deactivated in the directory. For internal or employee-oriented scenarios, this resolves a major security requirement. Further, by centralizing the issuance of access tokens, the security team can audit and even control the policies independent of API development.

Consumption Tracking

As we move further away from the hard technical implementation and into the business concerns and requirements, the next area is consumption management, or more fundamentally onboarding and engagement. To expose these functions, most API management platforms include a developer portal for documentation and samples, a logging page to show usage and errors for debugging, and sample code to show how to use the API. Every component here has exactly one goal: How can a developer get started with and use your API successfully?

Business Goals

The final aspect that an API management platform addresses are the business goals. On a technical layer, this overlaps with the consumption aspects to track overall API usage but provides a more detailed look at business analytics. Therefore, it's not just overall API consumption but identifying which API calls are the most and least important and how they map to revenue. The most advanced gateways will also include integration with web analytics platforms to track and understand where your users are struggling on setup and configuration.

Solutions Provided by an API Management Platform

An API management platform or an API gateway makes basic security easier. With a well-configured gateway, you know exactly which endpoints are open to the world and what parameters they expect. You still have to filter and validate the input according to best practices, but the attack surface is a fraction of what it would be otherwise.

An API management platform handles traffic shaping. Bad actors will misuse and abuse our API. There will also be people who make honest mistakes and run an infinite loop, as well as customers who are really excited about the service. Any one of those can take down our API or drive costs astronomically high. Regardless of the reason, we need to be able to throttle and stop traffic before it hurts us and our customers.

An API management platform lets you worry about other problems. Most teams have enough problems designing, building, documenting, demonstrating, and marketing an API. When we can hand off essential components to reliable third parties, we have to consider it so we can do all the tasks unique to us.

Finally, an API management platform is excellent at logging. One of the biggest challenges for both your customers and your team is understanding "what happened?" The gateways will capture everything and most present it in a clear, consistent manner. A good debugger will save developers - both internal and external - hours of effort and frustration.

Problems Your API Management Platform Won't Solve

An API management platform does not design your API. You still need to understand your users, their goals, and the best way to accomplish those goals. That will require you to determine which use cases you are and are not solving with your API. Further, you have to decide the name and structure of appropriate endpoints and what is required to interact with them.

An API management platform is also not a universal security solution. While it limits your attack surface to pre-defined endpoints with specified parameters, those endpoints still need adhere to security practices regarding data filtering, rate limiting, authentication, and authorization. Various API breaches - such as Equifax and Panera - resulted from attackers using published endpoints in unexpected ways to download entire customer lists, transaction history, and complete credit reports. Rate limiting would have slowed these attacks and monitoring may have detected them, but only strongly defined and enforced authentication and authorization could have stopped them.

The success of your API is also not driven by your API management platform. From a technical perspective, your API still has to be stable and reliable. From a product/market fit perspective, your API still has to solve an important problem for a measurable customer base. And finally, from a user experience perspective, your customers need to find your API and be able to get started quickly enough to solve their problem.

And finally, an API management platform will not establish governance policies for you. When large companies begin an API program or begin to coordinate API efforts, you have to create and enforce policies for tracking APIs lifecycle and development, consistent and predictable naming of endpoints and parameters, understanding and applying security procedures, and publishing them for each audience. These are all leadership and management issues you need to consider in addition to API gateway.

API Management Platform Comparison

This is a much more complex question and depends on your use case, budget, and familiarity. If your infrastructure is entirely on AWS, Azure, or Google Cloud, using their respective gateways is a safe choice.

If you are like most organizations and have various components and systems in various places, the decision becomes more challenging. Mulesoft has its roots in the Enterprise Service Bus (ESB) area, so it is ideal when you have to wrap existing systems and orchestrate components into a single interface. Apigee was born and lives entirely in the cloud so if your architecture is entirely in the cloud or you're just starting, it may be a better fit. Alternatively, Kong and Tyk.io are self-hosted open source gateways which will allow you to deploy them on nearly any architecture. If you're deep into microservices, they may be a better approach to embed directly into the microservice.

Regardless, the original constraints around access management don't go away. Having a central place to create, manage, audit, and deploy access and security policies is key to knowing your people and systems have the right access to the right systems for the right reasons for the right amount of time. Distributing that aspect across servers, teams, and codebases is confusing at best and catastrophic at worst.

○ ○ ○ ○ ○

About the Authors

Lee Brandt

Lee Brandt has spent two decades writing software professionally (and a few years unprofessionally before that), and he continues to learn every day. He has led teams in small and large companies and always manages to keep the business needs at the forefront of software development efforts and is currently a developer advocate at Okta. He speaks internationally about software development, from both a technical and business perspective, and loves to teach others what he learns. Lee writes software in Objective-C, JavaScript, and C#... mostly. He is a Microsoft Most Valuable Professional in Visual Studio and Development Technologies and one of the directors of the Kansas City Developer Conference (KCDC). Lee is also a decorated Gulf War veteran, a husband, a proud pet parent, and loves to play the drums whenever he gets any spare time.

Keith Casey

Keith Casey currently serves on the platform team at Okta working on the Identity and Authentication APIs. Previously, he served as an early developer evangelist at Twilio and before that worked on the Ultimate Geek Question at the Library of Congress. His underlying goal is to get good technology into the hands of good people to enable great things. In his spare time, he helps build and support the Austin tech community, blogs at caseysoftware.com and is fascinated by monkeys. He is also a co-author of A Practical Approach to API Design *(https://leanpub.com/restful-api-design)* from Leanpub.

Randall Degges

Randall Degges leads developer advocacy at Okta where he builds open source security libraries and helps make the Internet a little safer. Randall joined Okta from Stormpath and in a prior life, he was the CTO of OpenCNAM, the largest Caller ID API service. In his free time, Randall geeks out on web best practices, explores new technologies, and spends an inordinate amount of time writing Python, Node, and Go. As a fun fact, Randall runs *ipify.org*, one of the largest IP lookup APIs which serves over 30 billion requests per month.

Brian Demers

Brian Demers is a developer advocate at Okta, helping developers write secure Java applications. Brian is a Project Management Committee member for the Apache Shiro security project. Brian spends much of his day contributing to open source projects in the form of writing code, tutorials, blogs, and answering questions. Along with typical software development, he also has a passion for fast builds and automation.

Joël Franusic

Joël Franusic is a hacker and programmer-at-arms at Okta, where his job is to make simple things simple and complex things possible. Joël is a fan of literate programming, interactive development environments, and computer history. One of Joël's goals in life is to make all software from all of history available for instant use by any programmer. In his spare time Joël enjoys reading books and exploring interesting corners of computer history by doing things like writing a DNS server, programming an IBM 1401 using punch cards, and extracting all GIFs from Wikipedia.

Les Hazlewood

Les Hazlewood has a passion for HTTP and REST standards, application security, and large-scale system design. After moving to Silicon Valley to create a tech company, he gained a keen understanding of the challenges and rewards of working with both people and cutting-edge technology. He tries to channel that knowledge into making software and Internet standards better for everyone. Les has been actively involved in open source for more than 15 years, committing or contributing to projects like the Spring Framework, JBoss, Apache Shiro, JJWT, and many more. He is a senior software architect at Okta as well as the Ion Hypermedia Working Group Chair and Apache Shiro Project Management Committee Chair, and the former co-founder and CTO of Stormpath, the first API-driven Identity Management SaaS. Les has a BS in Computer Science from Georgia Tech and practices Kendo and studies Japanese when he's not coding.

Sai Maddali

Sai Maddali is a product manager on Okta's directories team where he is helping build the platform for customers to connect to Okta from various sources. He's spent his entire career in the identity space, coming to Okta from Stormpath where he worked as an engineer supporting developer success, and helped onboard developers to Stormpath's API and SDKs. Sai has a BS in Computer Engineering from Georgia Tech and is passionate about all things identity and user experience. He spends his free time doing street photography centered around people and their identities. You can find Sai on *Medium* and Twitter as *@saimaddali.*

Matt Raible

Matt Raible is a well-known figure in the Java community and has been building web applications for most of his adult life. For over 20 years, he has helped developers learn and adopt open source frameworks and use them effectively. He's a web developer, Java Champion, and developer advocate at Okta. Matt has been a speaker at many conferences worldwide, including Devoxx Belgium, Devoxx France, Jfokus, and JavaOne. He is the author of The JHipster Mini-Book, Spring Live, and contributed to Pro JSP. He is frequent contributor to open source and a member of the JHipster development team. You can find Matt online at *https://raibledesigns.com* and *@mraible* on Twitter.